A Field Guide to Prophetic Ministry

JOSH LAWRENCE

Copyright © 2016 Josh Lawrence

All rights reserved.

ISBN: 9780692614013

SPECIAL THANKS TO THESE GUYS AND THEIR RESOURCES

Approaching the Heart of Prophecy - Graham Cooke

Basic Prophetic Training – Kris Vallotton

School of the Prophets – Kris Vallotton

www.StreamsMinistries.com – John Paul Jackson

Basic Training for Prophetic Activations – Dan McCollam

Translating God – Shawn Bolz

Elijah Encounter - David Jonas

PURPOSE OF THIS HANDBOOK

This handbook is not meant to be strictly academic. Nor is it all inclusive. It is meant to provide some details and insight into the prophetic ministry so that you yourself may be able to explore it deeper. My prayer is that this will train and equip you to go deeper into the heart of the Father and display Him to the world around you.

TABLE OF CONTENTS

The Basics	9
The Language of Heaven	23
The Word of Knowledge	41
The Seer Realm	55
How to Receive a Prophetic Word	71
Dreams	85
Common Symbols and Interpretations	97
Growing in the Prophetic	107
Overcoming Fear and Rejection	118
Prophetic Guidelines	121

THE BASICS

I want to start out this manual by talking about hearing God. I know that most, if not all of you reading this manual, in some capacity can hear God. That being said, I just want to write briefly about the subject to create some context for other places we are going through the rest of this manual.

The rise and fall of every relationship can be traced back to one thing. Communication. Whether it is between a husband and a wife, coworkers, parents and children, business partners, whatever the relationship is, it hinges on one thing. It hinges on communication. Communication is a two way street. As Christians we often slip into seasons of our life when we go to God in prayer already with an agenda. As we pray we check off the items on our list and then go about the day as if God isn't an actual person but a magic genie to be summoned when we are in need. This manual deals primarily with the prophetic ministry as a lifestyle, but your ability to hear God for others will only come unless you can first hear him for yourself and your life.

How do we do "hear" God? It is simple really, expect Him to speak into everything. Expect that He has an opinion on everything we do and learn to value His opinion and His input. The more you open yourself up for communication the more you will find yourself communicating with Him.

One thing that we have learned is that God doesn't always speak to us plainly. If everything He said was made very clear and was "writing on the wall" so to speak, our responsibility for acting on what was made plain would be really high. Its like the quote from Spiderman, "With great power come great responsibility". Well, with great clarity on what God is saying, comes great responsibility to carry it out or act on it. God speaks to us in a language that requires us to hunger. We see in the New Testament Jesus would often speak in parables and almost intentionally confuse people or offend people to find out who the hungry ones are. He would have massive crowds around Him and then make a statement like this in John 6:54:

that whoever eats His flesh and drinks His blood will have eternal life.

With one statement, He would be standing there alone again, only to find out who the hungry ones were? He would know who was hungry, because those were the ones who would stick around and find out what His statement really means.

Don't be frustrated if you don't have the clarity you want. God is shaping that and forming that clarity in each of us. Every aspect of how He communicates with you is only discovered, searched out, and found out by trial and error.

One good thing to always do is to always ask two questions. These two questions were asked on the day of Pentecost: "What does this mean?" And "What must I do?" NEVER ask the why question because the why question will never be answered here on earth. Zechariah in Luke chapter 1, asked the why and look what did it get him? He lost his ability to communicate.

The Basics of Prophecy

Prophecy at its core is to first hear from God and then speak out what He is saying. Prophecy can include predicting future events or "foresight." It can also include hearing from the Lord and speaking things into existence or "forth sight."

> *The testimony of Jesus is the Spirit of prophecy (Revelation 19:10).*

All true prophecy is the testimony of Jesus; it comes from Him and it draws people to Him.

The purpose of the gift of prophecy in the New Testament church is described in 1 Corinthians:

> *But one who prophesies speaks to men for edification and exhortation and consolation (1 Corinthians 14:3).*

Edification means "to build up." Exhortation means "to call near." Consolation means "to cheer up."

In the New Testament Church, we as prophetic people are not called to bring negative words, correction or call fire down upon people. We are beacons of grace, not bringers of judgment. As New Testament believers, we are not called to prophesy the problem; we are called to prophesy the solutions. We are to call out the gold God has hidden in each and every person.

Have you ever been on the receiving end of a bad prophetic experience? If so, how did you feel after?

_____
_____
_____

What could you learn from your bad experience to help you prophesy to others in the future?

_____
_____
_____

Prophecy is a Gift

Prophecy is a gift, not a reward. The Bible tells us to earnestly desire the gifts. There is nothing we can do to earn the gift of prophecy. Neither is the gift of prophecy a mark of spiritual maturity; you do not have to wait to earn them. We do not earn the gift of prophecy. Just like any gift, you get it by receiving. The main way the Bible talks about receiving things in the spiritual sense is by asking (Matt. 7:7).

"Gift" or "charisma" means "a favor in which one receives without any merit on his own, a gift of divine grace." God is a good Father who loves to give good gifts to his children!

Imagine a child coming down for Christmas seeing many presents wrapped and laid under the tree waiting to be opened. A good father lives for these moments as he sees his children unwrapping the presents. So our Heavenly Father loves to see us un-wrap the gifts of the Spirit!

If you then, being evil, know how to give good gifts to your children, how much more will your Father who is in heaven give what is good to those who ask Him! (Matt 7:11).

For years the gifts of the Spirit have been taught that we need to find our one special gift. This results in the assumption that if we are not operating in a gift presently then we must not have that gift. This incorrect doctrine was based from the following verses, especially verse 1: "Distributing to each one individually just as He wills."

> *Now there are varieties of gifts, but the same Spirit. And there are varieties of ministries, and the same Lord. There are varieties of effects, but the same God who works all things in all persons. But to each one is given the manifestation of the Spirit for the common good. For to one is given the word of wisdom through the Spirit, and to another the word of knowledge according to the same Spirit; to another faith by the same Spirit, and to another gifts of healing by the one Spirit, and to another the effecting of miracles, and to another prophecy, and to another the distinguishing of spirits, to another various kinds of tongues, and to another the interpretation of tongues. But one and the same Spirit works all these things, distributing to each one individually just as He wills (1 Corinthians 12:4-11).*

Many Christians, especially operating in the five-fold offices carry a strong anointing in certain gifts. Just because someone has a strong anointing in a certain gift does not stop us from operating in the other eight gifts. The gifts of the Spirit, all nine of them, are distributed to us as we need them. Every believer has the potential to operate in every gift.

Since all gifts are available to us, we "learn" to walk in them. We have spent our lives operating in the natural world. We must learn to operate in the gifts of the Spirit and the gift of prophecy just as we learned to walk and talk as children.

The Role of Prophecy in Scripture

From Genesis to Revelation God was always speaking to mankind. God speaks to mankind through dreams, visions, angels and through prophets. Kings were anointed and humbled. The life of Jesus was foretold in many scriptures in the OT, from his birth to his death and resurrection each being fulfilled. Jesus was completely dependent upon hearing the voice of God (only speaking what he heard the father saying).

God is Always Speaking

Jesus is called "The Word" in the book of John; He lives within us and He is always speaking.

> Many, O Lord my God are the wonders, which You have done, And Your thoughts toward us; there is none to compare with You. If I would declare and speak of them, they would be too numerous to count (Psalms 40:5).

Every believer is prophetic to a degree. A believer is prophetic simply by knowing Jesus. Most people, once they are trained in the prophetic, realize that they had been hearing the voice of God all along, but never recognized it.

Prophetic training allows us to tune our spiritual ears to hear what the Lord is saying. Jesus said, "He who has ears to hear, let him hear" (Luke 8:8). This implies two things: first, that Jesus is speaking and second, some do not have their spiritual ears tuned into what He is saying.

God is always speaking but His word is hidden. God's word is hidden from the proud and is made available to ones who are humble and hungry for His word, those with a child-like faith.

> ...At that very time He rejoiced greatly in the Holy Spirit, and said, "I praise You, O Father, Lord of heaven and earth, that You have hidden these things from the wise and intelligent and have revealed them to infants. Yes, Father, for this way was well-pleasing in Your sight" (Luke 10:21-22).

> *It is the glory of God to conceal a matter, but the glory of kings is to search out a matter (Proverbs 25:2).*

As the Body of Christ, we are a chosen generation, a royal priesthood made to be prophetic.

> *To you it has been granted to know the mysteries of the kingdom of heaven, but to them it has not been granted (Matthew 13:11).*

God is always speaking, but His language in not only English. We must learn to tune our ears to hear by the Spirit.

All Believers Can Prophesy

When Paul said, "We may all prophesy," that includes everyone! As we draw nearer to Jesus in faith we will find there is an ease with which the believer can hear the voice of God. Prophetic, revelatory experiences are for everybody.

> *For you can all prophesy one by one, so that all may learn and all may be exhorted (1 Corinthians 14:31).*

The Apostle Paul said that we should earnestly desire spiritual gifts, especially the gift of prophecy. In other words, we should place a high value on the gift of prophecy, the ability to rightly hear the voice of God.

> *Pursue love, yet desire earnestly spiritual gifts, but especially that you may prophesy (1 Corinthians 14:1-2).*

> *Therefore, my brethren, desire earnestly to prophesy, and do not forbid to speak in tongues (1 Corinthians 14:39-40).*

According to the prophet Joel we are a prophetic generation that will hear God's voice. This is God's dream. In the book of Acts, Peter said, "This is that which was spoken of by the prophet Joel."

It will come about after this, that I will pour out My Spirit on all mankind; And your sons and daughters will prophesy, Your old men will dream dreams, Your young men will see visions. Even on the male and female servants, I will pour out My Spirit in those days (Joel 2:28-29).

The Secret Place - The Vital Key to the Prophetic

The greatest and most important key to Prophetic Ministry is a personal, intimate relationship with Jesus Christ. As we seek His face we hear His voice. Whoever belongs to Jesus communicates with Him. Knowing Him is our greatest call. It is possible to operate in the gift of prophecy as stated in Matthew.

Many will say to Me on that day, "Lord, Lord, did we not prophesy in Your name, and in Your name cast out demons, and in Your name perform many miracles?" And then I will declare to them, "I never knew you" (Matthew 7:22-23).

You and I never want to be in that group. How terrible that would be to work for Him, prophesy in His name, but never really know Him. I believe this is a major reason why the prophetic ministry has been abused and has brought upon the prophetic much controversy.

Now therefore, I pray You, if I have found favor in Your sight, let me know Your ways that I may know You, so that I may find favor in Your sight. Consider too, that this nation is Your people. And He said, "My presence shall go with you, and I will give you rest." Then he said to Him, "If Your presence does not go with us, do not lead us up from here. For how then can it be known that I have found favor in Your sight, I and Your people? Is it not by Your going with us, so that we, I and Your people, may be distinguished from all the other people who are upon the face of the earth?" (Exodus 33:13-16).

Our foremost cry should be as Moses cried, "Let me know Your ways that I may know You." The Lord will entrust Himself to the prophets to the extent that He will do "nothing unless He reveals His secret counsel to His servants the prophets" (Amos 3:7). The Lord will share His secrets to His friends simply because He wants to.

As we behold the glory of the Lord in the secret place, we become like Him, we become intimate with Him. This is when we begin to know His ways and become like Him. We call this "Beholding and Becoming." As we gaze upon Him, we become like Him.

Now the Lord is the Spirit, and where the Spirit of the Lord is, there is liberty. But we all, with unveiled face, beholding as in a mirror the glory of the Lord, are being transformed into the same image from glory to glory, just as from the Lord, the Spirit (2 Corinthians 3:17-18).

My Sheep Hear My Voice

My sheep hear My voice, and I know them, and they follow Me; and I give eternal life to them, and they will never perish (John 10:27-28).

When Samuel came to Jesse's house to anoint a king, David was out tending the sheep. The sheep would spend a lot of time with their shepherd until they would learn to recognize the voice of their shepherd above any other voice. Jesus uses this example to show us how in the secret place, we will learn to recognize His voice above all others, above the voice of our own desires of our soul and the voice of the enemy.

An anointed man or woman of God can lay hands on you and impact a grace for the gift of prophecy. But it is impossible for that person to impart unto you their relationship or their history with God. It is the requirement of every believer to develop his or her own relationship and history with God. That is done in the secret place where no one is watching.

Placing Value on the Prophetic

Our growth and maturity in the prophetic will be a result of how much we earnestly desire and contend for this gift. The words "earnestly desire" mean to "lust after." God wants to place an extremely high value and make room for the prophetic in our lives.

> *It is the Spirit who gives life; the flesh profits nothing; the words that I have spoken to you are spirit and are life (John 6:63-64).*

> *Man shall not live by bread alone, but on every word that proceeds out of the mouth of God (Matthew 4:4).*

> *So faith comes from hearing, and hearing by the word of Christ (Romans 10:17).*

> *Delight yourself in the Lord; And He will give you the desires of your heart (Psalm 37:4).*

> *...for where your treasure is, there your heart will be also (Matthew 6:21).*

Prophetic Community

A prophetic community happens when a group of people comes together in unity with a desire to hear the voice of God. This creates a high level prophetic anointing in a geographic location. An "umbrella of anointing" in the atmosphere is created causing even non-prophetic people to prophesy. This happened to Saul when he encountered the company of prophets;

When they came to the hill there, behold, a group of prophets met him; and the Spirit of God came upon him mightily, so that he prophesied among them. It came about, when all who knew him previously saw that he prophesied now with the prophets, that the people said to one another, "What has happened to the son of Kish? Is Saul also among the prophets?" (1 Samuel 10:10-12).

A Prophetic Community cultivates a prophetic lifestyle.

A Prophetic Community allows people to walk in their full potential of their prophetic calling. People are not judged by their limitations, but they are seen for their potential.

Iron sharpens iron; we grow faster in the prophetic as we grow together.

It's a group of people with relationship and accountability to each other and to leadership.

Developing a Culture of Risk within a Prophetic Community:

- Misses and mistakes are learning experiences and not shameful. We may fail a lot. It is better to swing and miss than not swing at all.
- There is no punishment for mistakes. We learn to fail successfully.
- Our goal is to be 100% accurate in prophetic ministry, yet realizing we are not yet there.
- We learn to be deeply accountable to each other in this lifestyle of risk.
- When people succeed we applaud them. When they fail, we pick them up and applaud them for stepping out in risk.
- A culture of risk will break a cycle of fear.
- Prophetic words are allowed to be tested in love, without causing offense.

Prophetic Activation

Pair up with someone you do not know very well.

1. Ask the Lord for one word for that person. Write down the first word that comes to your mind.

2. Ask the Lord to show you a picture in your mind that relates to that person. Write down the description of the first image you see.

Prophetic Challenge

Prophesy your day. Start your day by asking the Holy Spirit to reveal events of that day to you. Quiet yourself, clear your mind and ask Him to show you in a vision, word or impression what will happen that day. Write your thoughts or vision down and at the end of your day check your list.

NOTES

THE LANGUAGE OF HEAVEN

God is always speaking and He has created us as sons and daughters to live from a place of intimate relationship and communication. Individually, every believer is prophetic and together, we are a prophetic generation. Yet many people do not recognize when He is speaking to them. God speaks in many different and unusual ways. Some of the ways that He speaks are quite dramatic and earth shaking. Other times His voice is very soft and subtle.

As we begin to learn how He speaks we will look at our past events of life and realize that He has always been speaking to us. When we realize this, we will be like Jacob and say, "Surely the Lord is in this place, and I did not know it."

The purpose of this lesson is to show some of the many different ways that God communicates and to inspire openness to hearing His voice.

Visions

A very common way the Lord communicates is through visions.

> *It will come about after this. That I will pour out My Spirit on all mankind; And your sons and daughters will prophesy. Your old men will dream dreams. Your young men will see visions (Joel 2:28).*

**This list is not all-inclusive, but provides a good starting point for describing known experiences.

Visions of the Mind, Internal Visions or Closed Visions – These are moving visions projected upon the screen of your mind or imagination. These visions can happen when your eyes are closed or open. Daniel had this type of vision when he saw an angel.

I was looking in the visions in my mind as I lay on my bed, and behold, an angelic watcher, a holy one, descended from heaven (Daniel 4:13).

Open or External Visions – This is a type of vision that we can see with our natural or open eye. These appear more real, more vivid, and more distinct and are impacting. They appear as a movie screen. You feel that you can reach out and touch the vision. The visions are received when your eyes are open and can continue when involved in other activities, such as driving a car. (Check out James Maloney's book – *The Panaramic Seer*).

Pictorial Vision – This is what most people see when they get a vision. A single image or snapshot is seen within the mind that becomes an entire revelation. Most people, prophetic or not, see images in their imagination as they process information. An example would be if a friend was talking about a red fire truck; we could "see" the picture of that red fire truck in our mind. The Lord will project images within our mind and as our minds are renewed and we have "the mind of Christ" our imagination becomes "sanctified" and we can more easily discern the images that are from the Lord. These visions can happen when your eyes are closed or open. Many prophets, when prophesying, are simply describing and interpreting an image or picture they are seeing within their "sanctified imagination."

Dreams

Dreams are a common way of communication from the Lord. In the book of Deuteronomy, prophets are also referred to as "Dreamer of Dreams." While dreaming, the Lord is able to by-pass the reasoning of our natural mind. When sleeping, we are not dealing with the questions in our mind; Is this God or is this just me thinking this?

Most people have dreams, but not all dreams are from the Lord. Even powerful dreams, which we remember when we wake, may not be from the Lord. Dreams can come from the flesh or soulish realm and there are spirits in the evil realm, which will speak to us even in our dreams.

Dreams from the Lord are important and have many purposes.

Indeed God speaks once, or twice, yet no one notices it. "In a dream, a vision of the night, when sound sleep falls on men, while they slumber in their beds, then He opens the ears of men, and seals their instruction, that He may turn man aside from his conduct, and keep man from pride; He keeps back his soul from the pit, and his life from passing over into Sheol (Job 33:14-18).

It does not necessarily mean you are prophetic if you have dreams. Interpreting dreams is what makes us prophetic. Understanding symbols, numbers and colors are very important to the interpretation of dreams. This is discussed in more detail in a later section.

Trances

Trances are like visions, except you completely lose consciousness of your surroundings. Trances take us out of our natural mind as we are overcome by the Spirit of God. They are like a dream-like state while we are awake. Trances are a vehicle that the Lord uses to take us into an encounter, such as a doctor will put you "under" before the operation.

The Greek word for trance is "ekstasis," which means a displacement of the mind, i.e. bewilderment, or "ecstasy." Trances can last any length of time, from a few seconds to several hours.

Trances seem to happen to underscore the importance of the message the Lord is communicating. The Lord took Peter into a trance for the purpose of changing the doctrine of the early church that the Gospel should be preached to the Gentiles:

> *I was in the city of Joppa praying; and in a trance I saw a vision, an object coming down like a great sheet lowered by four corners from the sky; and it came right down to me, and when I had fixed my gaze on it and was observing it I saw the four-footed animals of the earth and the wild beasts and the crawling creatures and the birds of the air. I also heard a voice saying to me, "Get up, Peter; kill and eat." But I said, "By no means, Lord, for nothing unholy or unclean has ever entered my mouth." But a voice from heaven answered a second time, "What God has cleansed, no longer consider unholy" (Acts 11:5-9).*

Angels

Angels are messengers of God. Throughout scripture angels would bring messages from the heavenly realm to men and women. They also minister to us, protect us, go before us, strengthen us, bring prophetic words for us to speak, bring spiritual gifts and release the glory of God.

We can see angels with our outward natural eyes or we can see them in our mind with the "eyes of our understanding."

Do not neglect to show hospitality to strangers, for by this some have entertained angels without knowing it (Hebrews 13:2-3).

An angel appeared to Phillip to tell him to get up to speak to the Ethiopian eunuch:

But an angel of the Lord spoke to Philip saying, "Get up and go south to the road that descends from Jerusalem to Gaza." So he got up and went; and there was an Ethiopian eunuch… (Acts 8:26-27).

An angel appeared to Paul concerning going to Rome:

For this very night an angel of the God to whom I belong and whom I serve stood before me saying, "Do not be afraid, Paul; you must stand before Caesar" (Acts 27:23-24).

The sight of angels to the early church had been so common that when Peter was released from prison and knocked on the door of the room where the apostles were they were more able to believe it was his angel than Peter!

When he knocked at the door of the gate, a servant-girl named Rhoda came to answer. When she recognized Peter's voice, because of her joy she did not open the gate, but ran in and announced that Peter was standing in front of the gate. They said to her, "You are out of your mind!" But she kept insisting that it was so. They kept saying, "It is his angel" (Acts 12:13- 15).

Visitations and the Audible Voice of the Lord

Visitations are supernatural encounters between the heavenly realm and man. They are usually life-changing events. Visitations by Jesus are biblical, even in the Old Testament:

> When I, Daniel, had seen the vision, I sought to understand it; and behold, standing before me was one who looked like a man (Daniel 8:15).

The Lord sometimes speaks in an audible outward voice as if someone is in the room speaking. Paul experienced this on the road to Damascus:

> ...suddenly a light from heaven flashed around him; and he fell to the ground and heard a voice saying to him, "Saul, Saul, why are you persecuting Me?" And he said, "Who are You, Lord?" And He said, "I am Jesus whom you are persecuting" (Acts 9:3-5).

Translations and Transportation

This is when your spirit is taken or caught away to another place to deliver a message or word. This occurred to Philip when he was done witnessing to the Ethiopian eunuch and was caught up to preach in another city:

> When they came up out of the water, the Spirit of the Lord snatched Philip away; and the eunuch no longer saw him, but went on his way rejoicing. But Philip found himself at Azotus (Acts 8:39-40).

Caught Up in the Spirit

Paul was caught up in the Spirit to the third heaven. He was not sure if his spirit had left his body.

> I know a man in Christ who fourteen years ago — whether in the body I do not know, or out of the body I do not know, God knows — such a man was caught up to the third heaven (2 Corinthians 12:2-3).

Out of body experiences are biblical! God still uses these types of experiences to speak today. While we cannot make these types of experiences happen, we can position ourselves and make ourselves available by removing doubt and unbelief. If we would only believe then all things are possible.

Mind Reading

Many think of the New Age when they hear mind reading, but mind reading is a prophetic gift that Jesus demonstrated many times. Did you ever know what a person is thinking? How did you know that? You were operating in your prophetic gift!

> *The scribes and the Pharisees were watching Him closely to see if He healed on the Sabbath, so that they might find reason to accuse Him. But He knew what they were thinking (Luke 6:7-8).*

> *But Jesus, knowing what they were thinking in their heart, took a child and stood him by His side (Luke 9:47).*

> *But He knew their thoughts and said to them, "Any kingdom divided against itself is laid waste; and a house divided against itself falls" (Luke 11:17).*

Tongues and Interpretation of Tongues

The gift of tongues is a language that is unknown to the speaker given by the Holy Spirit. It is the words of the Holy Spirit spoken by a believer. We are not talking about the believer's prayer language, but a message to a person or congregation that requires interpretation.

> *For to one is given the word of wisdom through the Spirit, and to another the word of knowledge according to the same Spirit; to another faith by the same Spirit, and to another gifts of healing by the one Spirit, and to another the effecting of miracles, and to another prophecy, and to another the distinguishing of spirits, to another various kinds of tongues, and to another the interpretation of tongues (1 Corinthians 12:8-11).*

The gift of interpretation of tongues is a supernatural understanding given by the Holy Spirit. Notice the scripture says the gift is an interpretation, not a translation. Have you ever heard someone give a long message in tongues and when the interpretation came it seemed much shorter? A translation would be a word by word meaning of what was spoken. The word "interpret" means to paraphrase the meaning. That is why a message in tongues can be long while the interpretation can be much shorter or vice versa.

Scripture

The Lord will speak to us daily as we read the Bible. As we read the Bible we can experience both the Logos and the Rhema word.

Logos - the entire written 31,173 verses of the Bible inspired by God given to man.

All Scripture is inspired by God and profitable for teaching, for reproof, for correction, for training in righteousness; so that the man of God may be adequate, equipped for every good work (2 Timothy 3:16-17).

Rhema - is a specific word, a creative word, a single promise or phrase that has a special anointing for you for a specific time. A Rhema word can be a verse that the Holy Spirit seemed to breathe upon just for you. The verse or phrase seems to become highlighted and jumps off the page to you.

When the Holy Spirit quickens a verse, stop and mediate on it, even speaking the verse aloud until it is made alive in you. Deposit this scripture in your heart so the Holy Spirit can use it in your life. He is speaking it directly to you.

Creation

Creation has a voice that declares the Glory of God. God uses creation to speak of himself.

> Let the rivers clap their hands. Let the mountains sing together for joy (Psalm 98:8).

> For since the creation of the world His invisible attributes, His eternal power and divine nature, have been clearly seen, being understood through what has been made, so that they are without excuse (Romans 1:20).

God can speak to us by using nature in prophetic acts. In the book of Numbers God spoke through His creation, Balaam's donkey:

> And the Lord opened the mouth of the donkey, and she said to Balaam, "What have I done to you, that you have struck me these three times?" (Numbers 22:28).

Prophetic Arts

More churches are including prophetic arts as part of their worship. Prophetic songs can flow forth in services. A spontaneous dance is actually a prophetic act that the Lord is using to speak. We encourage painting and drawings in the Glory. The artist will receive an image or picture in their mind and paint it as the Lord is revealing His word through art.

> Then the virgin will rejoice in the dance, and the young men and the old, together, for I will turn their mourning into joy, and will comfort them and give them joy for their sorrow (Jeremiah 31:13).

> Let the word of Christ richly dwell within you, with all wisdom teaching and admonishing one another with psalms and hymns and spiritual songs, singing with thankfulness in your hearts to God (Colossians 3:16-17).

Verbal Communication

The Lord can speak to us through others without that person realizing they are giving a prophetic word. Watch for the anointing on a word or the "bubbling up" of the prophetic word.

Flashbacks

The Lord speaks to us in ways we can understand. In scripture Jesus often told parables and used examples that related to the people He was speaking to. When Jesus told a parable about sheep, they could relate to that.

The Lord can use past events from our life to speak to us or to give us understanding when delivering a prophetic word. For example, you could be delivering a prophetic word to someone and suddenly a memory of a past event may spring forth in your mind. Stop and ask the Lord for understanding. If that event created a sense of fear in you, the Lord could be showing you what that person is experiencing or experienced.

Impressions

Impressions are an inward witness of the Holy Spirit. An impression is not a voice but a "knowing" or a "feeling" about something. Impressions are a common way that the Lord communicates.

For it seemed good to the Holy Spirit and to us to lay upon you no greater burden than these essentials (Acts 15:28-29).

The importance of knowing the Holy Spirit in fellowship and as your best friend becomes clear as we begin to interpret our impressions. Our desires can be so strong they can be confused with our "inner witness." When we become so intimate with the Lord that we know His heartbeat, our heart begins to beat in unison with His. As we become established in His presence we will experience a much greater understanding and revelation.

Physical Impressions In the Body

We can receive words of knowledge about pain and sickness by causing the prophetic person to experience a pain or sensation within their body which correlates to the sicknesses of others. We learn to distinguish this by performing a "body check" and becoming aware of pains that are not ours.

Still Small Voice

I would like to give credit to parts of this section to *How to Hear God's Voice*, by Mark and Patti Virkler. I highly recommend that study to anyone wanting a greater understanding of how to hear the voice of God.

> *Then He said, "Go out, and stand on the mountain before the Lord." And behold, the Lord passed by, and a great and strong wind tore into the mountains and broke the rocks in pieces before the Lord, but the Lord was not in the wind; and after the wind an earthquake, but the Lord was not in the earthquake; and after the earthquake a fire, but the Lord was not in the fire; and after the fire a still small voice (1 Kings 19:11-12).*

With all the ways God can speak to man, He often speaks in the still small voice from within our spirit. This can start as a passing thought, word or impression. Often we dismiss or skip over His voice by not understanding it is the Lord speaking. We must train ourselves to recognize His still small voice, stop and capture His voice when He speaks.

Imagine the scene of two lovers whispering sweet things into each other's ears. There is no need to yell at each other because they are so close. This is a perfect picture of the Lord's still small voice. When we discover a love relationship with the King of Kings we will be awakened to direct encounters with Him and His still small voice will become a daily part of our life.

Below are truths that will help you recognize His still small voice:

There is someone living inside of you!

Or do you not know that your body is a temple of the Holy Spirit who is in you, whom you have from God, and that you are not your own? For you have been bought with a price (1 Corinthians 6:19-20).

But the one who joins himself to the Lord is one spirit with Him (1 Corinthians 6:17).

The spirit of man is the lamp of the Lord (Proverbs 20:27).

Abide in Me, and I in you (John 15:4).

I have been crucified with Christ; and it is no longer I who live, but Christ lives in me (Galatians 2:20).

All thoughts are not our thoughts.

We must come to terms that the Holy Spirit is living inside of us and there is going to be evidence of His presence. This is an incredible revelation! While some thoughts are completely ours, there are some that are supernatural. Some come from our mind and others come from the spirit world.

Remember that God is always speaking. Unless we learn to distinguish His thoughts from ours we will just group all thoughts together thinking they are our thoughts. Let's look at the three sources of thoughts or voices and learn how to distinguish the source.

Our thoughts – these are analytical and cognitive. An example would be when we wake up in the morning we mentally plan our day, making mental notes of appointments, work schedules, house cleaning, seeing friends, etc. We live this way out of our reasoning process. The thoughts are limited by our own knowledge, wisdom, understanding and abilities.

Holy Spirit thoughts – since these are not our thoughts, they are spontaneous. They flow from the river of the Holy Spirit who lives inside of us. Jesus said that out of our heart will flow rivers of living water. These spontaneous thoughts come from that river. All believers have these thoughts. As we grow in the prophetic we simply learn to "tune" into this flow. Have you ever wondered why a random thought that is not related to anything you are thinking of at the time springs forth to the top of your mind? These thoughts are often gentle and "light" upon our mind. They speak of His character: Edifier, Comforter, Teacher, Counselor, Healer and Giver of Life.

Thoughts from the enemy – since these are not our thoughts, they are spontaneous. They are destructive, evil and perverted. You can recognize these thoughts because they line up with the character of satan. He is a liar, destroyer, thief, murderer, and accuser. Do not accept guilt for evil thoughts, they are only temptations from the enemy. Sin becomes a reality when we open the door of our heart to those thoughts.

Fours Keys to Hearing God's Still Small Voice:

- Recognize God's voice as spontaneous thoughts come into your mind.
- Quiet yourself so you can hear God's Voice.
- Look for vision as you pray.
- Journal or write your prayers and God's answers.

Activation

We are going to practice positioning ourselves to hear the "still small voice" of God. Remember, God is always speaking and we are going to learn to tune into the flow of living water within us. Pair up with someone you are not familiar with.

1. Quiet yourself.
2. Pray and ask God to give you a prophetic word or picture for that person.
3. Quiet yourself again.
4. Look for vision. Believe that the next spontaneous thought or image will be from the Lord.
5. Now deliver the mail!

Prophetic Challenge

1. Prophesy to someone during the week using the steps described in the activation process. This can be done to anyone from your family, work, school, etc. If you know you are going to meet a specific person ask the Lord before the meeting. Write the word down. You do not have to be "preachy"; in fact, you do not even have to tell the person that it is a prophetic word. You can work the prophetic word into your general conversation and watch the expression on the person's face.
2. Begin journaling your prophetic encounters, thoughts and words from the Lord. Begin by quieting yourself and getting still. Ask Jesus to speak to you, and then tune to the flowing thoughts and pictures. Ask Jesus questions, such as "What do You think of me?" "What do You love about me?" "What is blocking me from having a deeper relationship with You?" Begin journaling.

An inaccurate prophetic word does not make that person a false prophet.

- Allow your mistakes and failures to be learning experiences.
- You will make mistakes, but God is bigger than your mistakes.
- Clean up your own messes. If you miss a word or said something in the moment that wasn't of God, you resolve it by going to the person and talking as laid out in Mathew 18.
- If a word involves direction, have an overseer involved in the application of the word.
- Prophecy can be a potential word and a conditional word.
- Strengthen, encourage and comfort.
- Invest in your prophetic education.
- Fear is a demonic spirit, defeat it in the name of Jesus.
- Resist condemnation. The enemy is an accuser.
- Resist the fear of making mistakes.
- Depend completely upon the Holy Spirit.

NOTES

THE WORD OF KNOWLEDGE

To each one is given the manifestation of the Spirit for the common good. To one is given through the Spirit the word of wisdom, and to another the word of knowledge according to the same Spirit (1 Corinthians 12:7, 8).

Pursue love, and earnestly desire the spiritual gifts, especially that you may prophesy (1 Corinthians 14:1).

Defined:

"This is the supernatural revelation of fact about a person or situation, which is not learned through the efforts of the natural mind, but is a fragment of knowledge freely given by God, disclosing the truth which the Spirit wishes to be made known concerning a particular person or situation." - John Wimber

A word of knowledge is a definite conviction, impression or divine knowing. It is a supernatural insight, understanding of circumstances, situations or problems, a knowing of what to do, a divine piece of information about the past or present.

Word of Knowledge vs. the Gift of Prophesy

"People often confuse the word of knowledge with the gift of prophecy. The word of knowledge describes something that took place in the past, a current circumstance, or a fact about someone's life. Sometimes when we prophesy, someone can mistakenly think that the prophecy wasn't accurate because it was not something that is currently happening, or has ever happened in that person's life. Pure prophesy is about the future. If the prophetic word lacks an element of something that has already taken place, this simply means that the word of knowledge was not part of the delivery. A word of knowledge is simply knowing a fact, revealed by the Holy Spirit, of which we had no prior knowledge." – Basic Training for the Prophetic Ministry, Kris Vallotton

Often a prophetic word can include both a Word of Knowledge (supernatural revelation of a past or current circumstance) and a Word of Prophecy (supernatural revelation of a future event). The Word of Knowledge can bring credibility to the Word of Prophecy. An example of this is when Jesus spoke to the woman at the well.

In the below passage, the Word of Knowledge is underlined and the Word of Prophecy is in bold:

> *The woman said to Him, "Sir, give me this water, so I will not be thirsty nor come all the way here to draw." He said to her, "Go, call your husband and come here." The woman answered and said, "I have no husband." Jesus said to her, <u>"You have correctly said, 'I have no husband'; for you have had five husbands, and the one whom you now have is not your husband; this you have said truly."</u> The woman said to Him, "Sir, I perceive that You are a prophet. Our fathers worshiped in this mountain, and you people say that in Jerusalem is the place where men ought to worship." Jesus said to her,* **"Woman, believe Me, an hour is coming when neither in this mountain nor in Jerusalem will you worship the Father. You worship what you do not know; we worship what we know, for salvation is from the Jews. But an hour is coming, and now is, when the true worshipers will worship the Father in spirit and truth; for such people the Father seeks to be His worshipers. God is spirit, and those who worship Him must worship in spirit and truth."** *The woman said to Him, "I know that Messiah*

is coming (He who is called Christ); when that One comes, He will declare all things to us." Jesus said to her, "I who speak to you am He" (John 4:15-26).

After the woman left Jesus she went into the city and told everyone, "Come, see a man who told me all the things that I have done." (John 4:29). This statement was not true as Jesus did not tell her "everything" she had done. The impact of the Word of Knowledge was that powerful!

Words of Knowledge in Scriptures:

1. Jesus Operating in Word of Knowledge:

Go into the village in front of you, where on entering you will find a colt tied, on which no one has ever yet sat. Untie it and bring it here. If anyone asks you, "Why are you untying it?" you shall say this: "The Lord has need of it" (Luke 19:30,31).

Go to the sea and cast a hook and take the first fish that comes up, and when you open its mouth you will find a shekel. Take that and give it to them (the tax collectors) for me and for yourself (Matthew 17:27).

Jesus saw Nathanael coming towards him and said of him, "Behold, an Israelite indeed in whom there is no deceit!" Nathanael said to him, "How do you know me? Jesus answered him, "Before Philip called you, when you were under the fig tree, I saw you" (John 1:47-50).

2. The Early Church Operating in the Word of Knowledge:

But a man named Ananias, with his wife Sapphira, sold a piece of property, and with his wife's knowledge he kept back for himself some of the proceeds and brought only a part of it and laid it at the apostles' feet. But Peter said, "Ananias, why has Satan filled your heart to lie to the Holy Spirit and to keep back for yourself part of the proceeds of the land?" (Acts 5:1-5).

And the Lord said to him, "Rise and go to the street called Straight, and at the house of Judas look for a man of Tarsus named Saul, for behold, he is praying and he has seen in a vision a man named Ananias come in and lay his hands on him so that he might regain his sight" (Acts 9:11-12).

What is it Lord? And He said to him, "Your prayers and your alms have ascended as a memorial before God. And now send men to Joppa and bring one Simon who is called Peter. He is lodging with one Simon a tanner, whose house is by the seaside" (Acts 10:4-6).

When I had returned to Jerusalem and was praying in the temple, I fell into a trance and saw Him saying to me, "Make haste and get out of Jerusalem quickly, because they will not accept your testimony about me" (Acts 22:17-21).

Word of Knowledge for Healing

The Word of Knowledge is a very effective tool for healing:

Unbelief

"Teacher, I brought my son to you for he has a spirit that makes him mute. And whenever it seizes him, it throws him down, and he foams and grinds his teeth and becomes rigid. So I asked your disciples to cast it out, and they were not able..." (Mark 9:17-29).

"All things are possible for one who believes." Immediately the father of the child cried out and said, "I believe, help my unbelief!" (Mark 9:23).

Demons

He rebuked the unclean spirit, saying to it, "You mute and deaf spirit, I command you, come out of him and never enter him again" (Mark 9:17-29).

Blind

Then a demon-oppressed man who was blind and mute was brought to him (Matthew 12:22).

Infirmity

And there was a woman who had a disabling spirit for eighteen years (Luke 13:11).

Depression

The garment of praise for the spirit of heaviness (Isaiah 61:3).

Sin

But finding no way to bring him in, because of the crowd, they went up on the roof and let him down with his bed through the tiles into the midst before Jesus. And when He saw their faith, He said, "Man, your sins are forgiven you. I say to you, rise, pick up your bed and go home" (Luke 5:17-26).

*Example: Unforgiveness can be a hindrance.

Activate the Person's Faith

On another Sabbath, He entered the synagogue and was teaching, and a man was there whose right hand was withered … and after looking around at them all He said to him was, "Stretch out your hand." And he did so, and his hand was restored (Luke 6:10).

*Example: Getting a man with bad knees to bend his knees to see if something is happening.

Compassion

When He went ashore He saw a great crowd, and He had compassion on them and healed their sick (Matthew 14:14).

*Example: Healing of a sick baby in the slums; you won't need a sermon on faith when the people see the demonstration of the gospel.

God's Love

For in Christ Jesus neither circumcision nor un-circumcision counts for anything, but only faith working through love (Galations 5:6).

Ways You Can Receive Words of Knowledge:

Feel It

- A sympathetic pain in some part of the body.
- A throbbing sensation.
- A strong emotion such as fear or panic.

See It

- Mental picture such as a body part, perhaps a heart, foot, etc.
- A picture of a person with a condition such as a limp.
- A crutch, wheelchair, eyeglasses
- An unusual item such as a paintbrush, bicycle, etc.

Read It

- A person with a word written across his body or above.
- May look like a newspaper headline, banner or sign.

Think It

- You may have a mental impression of a condition.

Say It

- While talking or praying the Holy Spirit starts speaking and you hear it for the first time.

Hear it

- Can be the still small voice.

Dream It

- You may have vivid dream of a person. God can speak to you at night while you are asleep so you can act upon it when you are awake.

Preparation to Awaken the Gift of the Word of Knowledge:

Believe

All things are possible to him that believes (Mark 9:23).

And these signs will accompany those that believe: in my name they will cast out demons (Mark 16:17).

Earnestly Desire

Pursue love, and earnestly desire the spiritual gifts, especially that you may prophesy (1 Corinthians 14:1).

Cleanse your Heart

If I had cherished iniquity in my heart, the Lord would not have listened (Psalm 66:18).

Sanctified Imagination

The eyes of your understanding being enlightened; that you may know what is the hope which He has called you, what are the riches of His glorious inheritance in the saints (Ephesians 1:18).

Practice

For you may all prophesy one by one, that all may learn and all may be encouraged (1 Colossians 14:31).

But solid food is for the mature, for those who have their powers of discernment trained by constant practice to distinguish good from evil (Hebrews 5:14).

No Fear

For this reason I remind you to fan into flame the gift of God, which is in you through the laying on of my hands, for God gave us a spirit not of fear but of power love and self-control (1 Timothy 1:6-7).

How to Deliver a Word of Knowledge

Let's review some practical ways of operating in the Word of Knowledge effectively. It is important to keep in mind that we are not perfect and there are times we may miss it. However, we do not want to bring damage to people's lives.

1. Model humility – we ourselves are human and may miss it. Even if you feel that you are 100% sure of your word, always be gentle and humble.

2. It is ok to be tentative in speaking out the word. Do not be afraid to admit that you are nervous. Speaking the Word of Knowledge in a strong manner does not make it more anointed.

3. Don't let your fear rob the person of their blessing. Someone once said that faith is spelled "R-I-S-K."

4. Avoid speaking negative words or words that may bring fear upon a person. Death and life are in the power of the tongue (Prov. 18:21). The Word of Knowledge, when handled properly, is of great value, but when handled improperly, can bring condemnation upon people.

5. Speak in natural tones, avoid hype. Avoid "Christianese" style of language. Practice as if you were speaking to someone outside of the church. Allow the supernatural power of God to flow from you without scaring people with "spiritual weirdness" or excess.

6. Ask the Lord for the right timing to deliver the Word of Knowledge that you have. Psalms 104:27 says; "They all wait for You, to give them their food in due season." God has a due season or a right timing when the people's heart has been properly prepared to receive.

7. The Word of Knowledge can come very quickly and vague. Press into the word asking the Lord for more revelation. The more specific the word, the more faith it will build.

8. Do not add your own interpretation or opinion. There is a difference between further revelation from the Lord and your own interpretation. The word you give may make no sense to you. Avoid the temptation to modify the word so that the word brings understanding to you.

9. Resist the thought that the word you have is not important or it is just you.

10. Remember, breath mints are anointed!

Activation

Practice in a group setting. Separate into groups of 4 to 6 people. Choose one member and have everyone prophesy to that person. Ask a member of the group to write down the prophetic words. After the person has received a prophetic word from each person in the group have the person who received the prophetic words to weigh and give feedback to the group.

Prophetic Challenge

Go to a restaurant with a group of prayer partners. Have each person write down 3 things that the Holy Spirit shows you about your server. Present it to your server in a non-religious way.

NOTES

A Field Guide to Prophetic Ministry

THE SEER REALM

Formerly in Israel, when a man went to inquire of God, he used to say, "Come, and let us go to the seer"; for he who is called a prophet now was formerly called a seer (1 Sam 9:9).

Nahbi Prophet vs. the Seer Prophet

Nahbi (naw-bee) – a prophet who declares the words of the Lord as he is given them. The Nahbi prophet often hears and repeats as he is spoken to by the Lord. He often receives revelation from the Lord in spontaneous faster flowing inspired thoughts or words. Sometimes the Nahbi prophet will use the gift of tongues and interpretation of tongues. When giving prophetic words the Nahbi prophet will often begin by saying, "I hear the Lord saying…"

Seer – a Seer prophet is one who emphasizes visions and the revelatory gifts verses the audible speaking gifts. A seer will often operate at a slower pace in the delivery of the prophetic word as they describe the pictures and images in their mind. The seer type relies heavily upon the presence of God and angelic visitation to initiate the revelatory realms. When giving prophetic words the seer will often begin by saying, "I see…"

The Importance of Developing the Seer Gift

Jesus, who was 100% God, came to earth as 100% man and modeled what ministry should look like when we are in total submission to the will of God. Not one miracle by

Jesus did He use his power as God, but as a man. The potential is available to each of us to do what Jesus did. This statement should provoke us to remove all sin, fear and unbelief in our life so we can draw nearer to Him. As we draw nearer to Him we will be able to "see" what He is doing and model that in our ministries.

100% Man:

> *Christ Jesus who existed in the form of God did not consider equality with God as something to be used to His advantage. Instead He emptied Himself by assuming the form of a slave, taking on the likeness of man. He had to go to the cross as a man to represent us as a man (Philippians 2:6).*

Jesus lived His life from a place of intimacy, an "inner relationship" with God, only speaking what He heard the Father saying and only doing what He saw the Father doing. Jesus lived a life without other options.

> *Truly, truly, I say to you, the Son can do nothing of Himself, unless it is something He sees the Father doing; for whatever the Father does, these things the Son also does in like manner (John 5:19).*

The Seer Gift is a restoration of our spiritual sight that we had in the garden

> *When the woman saw that the tree was good for food, and that it was a delight to the eyes, and that the tree was desirable to make one wise (Genesis 3:6).*

After they ate from the tree and fell into sin, note that the scriptures say that their eyes were opened. The eyes that were opened were due to the knowledge of good and evil or sin.

> *...she took from its fruit and ate; and she gave also to her husband with her, and he ate. Then the eyes of both of*

> *them were opened, and they knew that they were naked; and they sewed fig leaves together and made themselves loin coverings (Genesis 3:6-7).*

Their eyes were opened, but they could not see the Lord walking in the garden with these open eyes; they lost spiritual sight.

> *They heard the sound of the Lord God walking in the garden in the cool of the day, and the man and his wife hid themselves from the presence of the Lord God among the trees of the garden (Genesis 3:8).*

These are other verses that support that the fall or sin has blinded our spiritual eyes:

> *For this reason they could not believe, for Isaiah said again, "HE HAS BLINDED THEIR EYES AND HE HARDENED THEIR HEART, SO THAT THEY WOULD NOT SEE WITH THEIR EYES AND PERCEIVE WITH THEIR HEART, AND BE CONVERTED AND I HEAL THEM" (John 12:39-40).*

> *But the one who hates his brother is in the darkness and walks in the darkness, and does not know where he is going because the darkness has blinded his eyes (1 John 2:11).*

Jesus came to reconcile us to the Father. The cross removed our sin and reconciled us to the intimate relationship man had with the Father at the garden. Jesus came to restore our spiritual sight and close our eyes that were opened due to sin and open our spiritual eyes.

> *And Jesus said, "For judgment I came into this world, so that those who do not see may see, and that those who see may become blind." Those of the Pharisees who were with Him heard these things and said to Him, "We are not blind too, are we?" Jesus said to them, "If you were blind, you would have no sin; but since you say, 'We see,' your sin remains" (John 9:39-41).*

How to See in the Spirit – Looking for Vision

Nebuchadnezzar and Daniel's experiences are important for us to learn how to press into vision. It is important to be comfortable in our hearts that God uses our minds to speak to us by His voice, visions and dreams.

> I, Nebuchadnezzar, was at ease in my house and flourishing in my palace. I saw a dream and it made me fearful; and these fantasies as I lay on my bed and the visions in my mind kept alarming me (Daniel 4:5).

> Now these were the visions in my mind as I lay on my bed: I was looking, and behold, there was a tree in the midst of the earth and its height was great (Daniel 4:10).

In the following verse Nebuchadnezzar sees an angel. He saw the angel in his mind. Seeing the angel in his mind is as real as if the angel was standing before him in the natural. We need to learn to try what we see in our mind.

> I was looking in the visions in my mind as I lie on my bed, and behold, an angelic watcher, a holy one, descended from heaven (Daniel 4:13).

Daniel's experience is another great example of when we see visions in our mind. They are real and of great importance.

> In the first year of Belshazzar, king of Babylon, Daniel saw a dream and visions in his mind as he lay on his bed; then he wrote the dream down and related the following summary of it (Daniel 7:1-3).

A vision began in Daniel's mind. Note how Daniel began to take an active role and posture himself to receive the vision and go deeper into the vision. When the vision started, Daniel turned aside, blocked out distractions and started "looking" into his vision.

> *I was looking in my vision by night, and behold, the four winds of heaven were stirring up the great sea. And four great beasts were coming up from the sea, different from one another (Daniel 7:2).*

Daniel continues to posture himself, concentrate on the vision and "keeps looking." As he does this, the vision unfolds and he is able to receive the fullness of what the Lord wants to show him.

> *The first was like a lion and had the wings of an eagle. I kept looking until its wings were plucked, and it was lifted up from the ground and made to stand on two feet like a man (Daniel 7:4).*

> *After this, I kept looking and behold, another one, like a leopard (Daniel 7:6).*

> *After this I kept looking in the night visions, and behold, a fourth beast (Daniel 7:7).*

By verse 9, Daniel has been pressing into his vision for some time now. As he continues to contend and press, he is taken into a throne room encounter with the Father. A vision can begin faintly. It is important to learn to press into our visions as we learn to develop our seer gift.

> *I kept looking until thrones were set up, and the Ancient of Days took His seat; His vesture was like white snow and the hair of His head like pure wool. His throne was ablaze with flames; Its wheels were a burning fire (Daniel 7:9).*

Daniel continues to press in and "look into his vision." Finally, in verse 13, he has an encounter with Jesus.

> *Then I kept looking because of the sound of the boastful words which the horn was speaking; I kept looking until the beast was slain, and its body was destroyed and given to the burning fire. As for the rest of the beasts, their dominion was taken away, but an extension of life was*

> *granted to them for an appointed period of time (Daniel 7:11-12).*

> *I kept looking in the night visions, and behold, with the clouds of heaven, One like a Son of Man was coming, and He came up to the Ancient of Days, and was presented before Him (Daniel 7:13).*

The Apostle John positioned himself to receive visions. We cannot make vision happen or imagine it on our own. We can however, position ourselves to receive visions from the Lord. John was caught up into a vision when he was in prayer and "in the Spirit." This further demonstrates that we play a part in receiving vision.

> *I was in the Spirit on the Lord's day, and I heard behind me a loud voice, like the sound of a trumpet, saying, "Write in a book what you see, and send it to the seven churches" (Revelation 1:10-11).*

> *After these things I looked, and behold, a door standing open in heaven, and the first voice which I had heard, like the sound of a trumpet speaking with me, said, "Come up here, and I will show you what must take place after these things." Immediately, I was in the Spirit; and behold, a throne was standing in heaven (Revelation 4:1-2).*

Another way to increase the value we place upon the thoughts and visions within our mind is to remember that God treats that which we see or think in our mind as real as the actual act.

> *You have heard that it was said, "YOU SHALL NOT COMMIT ADULTERY," but I say to you that everyone who looks at a woman with lust for her has already committed adultery with her in his heart (Matthew 5:27-29).*

> *You have heard that the ancients were told, "YOU SHALL NOT COMMIT MURDER" and "Whoever commits murder shall be liable to the court." But I say to you that everyone*

who is angry with his brother shall be guilty before the court (Matthew 5:21-22).

The Transfiguration – A Vision

The Transfiguration was when the three disciples saw Jesus with Elijah and Moses. This event was called a vision! A vision of the mind from God can transform your life.

Six days later Jesus took with Him Peter and James and John His brother, and led them up on a high mountain by themselves. And He was transfigured before them; and His face shone like the sun, and His garments became as white as light. And behold, Moses and Elijah appeared to them, talking with Him. Peter said to Jesus, "Lord, it is good for us to be here. If You wish, I will make three tabernacles here: one for You, and one for Moses, and one for Elijah." While he was still speaking, a bright cloud overshadowed them, and behold, a voice out of the cloud said, "This is My beloved Son, with whom I am well-pleased; listen to Him!" When the disciples heard this, they fell face down to the ground and were terrified. And Jesus came to them and touched them and said, "Get up, and do not be afraid." And lifting up their eyes, they saw no one except Jesus Himself alone.

As they were coming down from the mountain, Jesus commanded them, saying, "Tell the vision to no one until the Son of Man has risen from the dead" (Matthew 17:1-9).

If you have a desire to experience more life changing visions and encounters in your life you simply need to ask.

Ask, and it will be given to you; seek, and you will find; knock, and it will be opened to you (Matthew 7:7).

Our Imagination was Created by God.

Our imagination is another word for using our mind. Our imagination is like an organ created by God so we can communicate with an unseen realm. Our imagination is our "spiritual eyes" or as the following verse refers to as the "eyes of our heart."

I pray that the eyes of your heart may be enlightened, so that you will know what is the hope of His calling, what are the riches of the glory of His inheritance in the saints (Ephesians 1:18).

When we think of our imagination most of us think of our childhood, imaginary friends, imagining situations and games when we played. Children love the imaginary realm and are easily engaged there.

We deal in the everyday realities of life and many of us have allowed the world to tell us that the use of our imagination is regarded as foolishness and should be reserved for children. Hence the phase, "Oh well, that is only your imagination!"

Whether we realize it or not, we use our imagination every day. Our imagination has been bombarded by the world and clouded with unholy images and by our experiences. Because of these thoughts we often are afraid to use or exercise our imagination. We can shut down our imagination and hinder our ability from hearing God rightly.

God created our imagination to communicate His specific plans and definite purposes in our lives. His will is made known to us because the imagination is the place where God most often speaks to us by dreams and visions. Actually, our imagination is a powerful path to prophetic revelation and destiny.

God wants us to develop a child-like faith. Bill Johnson wrote a book called, *Dreaming with God*. It takes a child-like faith to allow ourselves to dream His dreams and see those dreams in our imagination.

Truly I say to you, unless you are converted and become like children, you will not enter the kingdom of heaven (Matthew 18:3-4).

Examples of the Use of a Sanctified Imagination:

Building of the Tabernacle

And the King(David) said to Nathan the prophet, "See now I dwell in a house of cedar, but the ark of God dwells within tent curtains." Nathan said to the King, "Go, do all that is within your mind, for the Lord is with you" (2 Samuel 7:2-3).

Tabernacle

Oh Lord God of Abraham, Isaac and of Israel, our fathers, keep this forever in the imagination of the thoughts of the heart of thy people, and prepare their hearts unto thee: And give to Solomon a perfect heart, to keep thy commandments, thy testimonies, and thy statutes, and to do all these things, and to build the palace for which I have made provision (1 Chronicles 29:18).

Prophetic Word for a Nation

The word of the Lord came to me saying, "What do you see, Jeremiah? " And I said, "I see a rod of an almond tree." Then the Lord said to me, "You have seen well, for I am watching over my word to perform it" (Jeremiah 1:11-12).

Direction for the Church

I was in the city of Joppa praying; and in a trance I saw a vision, an object coming down like a great sheet, lowered by four corners from the sky; and it came right down to me; and when I fixed my gaze on it and was observing it I saw the four footed animals of the earth and the wild beasts and the crawling creatures and the birds of the air (Acts 11:5-10).

Direction for Evangelism

A vision appeared to Paul in the night: a man of Macedonia was standing and appealing to him, and saying, "Come over to Macedonia to help us" (Acts 16:9).

Seeing in Heavenly Realms

After these things I looked, and behold, a door standing open in heaven, and the first voice which I heard, like the sound of a trumpet speaking with me, said, "Come up here, and I will show you what must take place after these things" (Revelation 4:1).

Faith to See

Many people, when referring to Enoch, say that he was taken to heaven and did not see death because he got so close to God, and God loved him so much. Actually the scriptures tell us Enoch was taken to heaven because of his faith. Our faith is powerful and is necessary to release the promises of heaven over our lives.

By faith, Enoch was taken up so that he would not see death; AND HE WAS NOT FOUND BECAUSE GOD TOOK HIM UP; for he obtained the witness that before his being taken up he was pleasing to God. And without faith it is impossible to please Him, for he who comes to God must believe that He is and that He is a rewarder of those who seek Him (Hebrews 11:5-6).

Our level of prophetic ability and gifting is determined by our faith. When we are believing to receive visions in the seer realm, we will!

Since we have gifts that differ according to the grace given to us, each of us is to exercise them accordingly: if prophecy, according to the proportion of his faith (Romans 12:6).

All things are possible to him who believes (Mark 9:23).

Therefore I say to you, all things for which you pray and ask, believe that you have received them, and they will be granted you (Mark 11:24).

Biblical Safeguard

Now suppose one of you fathers is asked by his son for a fish; he will not give him a snake instead of a fish, will he? Or if he is asked for an egg, he will not give him a scorpion, will he? If you then, being evil, know how to give good gifts to your children, how much more will your heavenly Father give the Holy Spirit to those who ask Him? (Luke 11:11-13).

Many people in the church have a fear of the new age movement and avoid anything that resembles the new age. This has caused many to shut down their imagination or the "eyes of our heart." The above verse from Luke is a covenant promise, which proclaims the promises of the Lord. If we ask the Lord for vision to see in the seer realm, we can be confident that the power of God to keep us safe is stronger than the power of the enemy to deceive us.

3 Steps into the Seer Realm

How do we posture ourselves to see visions and operate in the seer realm? Ask God to baptize you with a fire of Holiness and remove the uncleanness of this world from you. Then press in, contend for a greater anointing in the seer realm. Finally, when the visions begin, trust they are from God and receive them like a child.

1. Matt 5:8 – "Blessed are the pure in heart, for they shall see God."
2. Matt 11:12 – "From the days of John the Baptist until now, the kingdom of heaven suffers violence, and violent men take it by force."
3. Mark 10:15 – "Truly I say to you, whoever does not receive the kingdom of God like a child will not enter it at all."

Activation

The Bible is meant to be experienced, not just read as history. Choose a scene in the Bible, play it within your mind with yourself inserted into the scene. Ask Jesus to speak to you through that encounter.

Prophetic Challenge

Practice activations daily that will allow God to restore your visionary capacity. Quiet your mind and ask the Lord to show you visions. A vision can come very faint, but focus and "keep looking" like Daniel did.

Meditate in your heart upon your bed, and be still (Psalm 4:4).

NOTES

A Field Guide to Prophetic Ministry

HOW TO RECEIVE PROPHETIC WORDS

Involvement in Prophetic Ministry means that since we will be around prophetic people, we will receive many prophetic words for ourselves. Accurately interpreting these words is important and our interpretation is not just a process of knowing scripture but also of having a transformed heart.

A transformed heart comes from not just "knowing about God," but "knowing God." Jesus said that as we "know Him" we are like sheep that will follow that voice and will not be deceived by the voice of a stranger.

Types of Prophetic Words

Prophetic words can be classified in three different categories:

Biblical Words – Words that have direct Biblical reference.

*Example: "I hear the Lord saying, 'Go into all the world and preach the Gospel.'"

Extra-Biblical Words – Prophetic utterances not explicitly stated in the Bible.

*Example: "I hear the Lord saying, 'You are to go to Africa and preach the Gospel.'"

Anti-Biblical Words – False words that are contrary to scripture.

*Example: "I hear the Lord saying, 'Divorce your spouse and go to Africa and preach the Gospel.'"

Guidelines for Judging Prophetic Words

- Don't stifle or despise prophecy, but test it. Always seek the Lord's guidance through prayer and meditations.
- When receiving a prophetic word, immediately turn to the Holy Spirit and ask Him what to do with what you have heard. The interpretation and application belongs to Him.
- The word must line up with the teaching and principles of scriptures as well as the heart of Father God.
- It must bear witness with the spirit of the one who receives it. Or is there a check in your spirit?
- The fruit of the prophetic word must be that the person receiving it is brought closer to God and His people.
- Compare the word against things God has spoken into your life through prior prophecies, personal devotions, pastoral counsel, etc.
- If you have any questions, alarm, fear or discomfort about a particular word, run it by your pastor or mentor. (Deut. 13:5)
- The word must edify and build up.
- Remember, "we prophecy in part" (1 Cor. 13:9). You may need further revelation on the word.
- Do not "read into" the word to make it what you want it to say.
- Do not act upon any predictive, directive words unless you have confirmation from other sources. Ask the Lord what His time frame is for the word.
- Beware of corrective, judgmental or condemning prophecy.(1 Cor. 14:3)

- Beware of prophesies that bring fear or confusion. (Romans 8:15)
- Prophetic words often bring clarification and confirmation.

Judging the Interpretation

It is easy to misjudge a prophetic word by missing the timing or the meaning of the prophecy. We can misjudge a prophetic word by our own limited understanding, opinions or biases.

If prophecy goes against or contradicts scripture, throw it out! However, the prophecy can be correct, but against our understanding of scripture.

An example of this is Peter's vision in Joppa:

> Peter went up on the housetop about the sixth hour to pray. But he became hungry and was desiring to eat; but while they were making preparations, he fell into a trance; and he saw the sky opened up, and an object like a great sheet coming down, lowered by four corners to the ground, and there were in it all kinds of four-footed animals and crawling creatures of the earth and birds of the air. A voice came to him, "Get up, Peter, kill and eat!" But Peter said, "By no means, Lord, for I have never eaten anything unholy and unclean" (Acts 10:9-14).

Peter's vision was a direct contradiction of laws taught in the OT, but the interpretation was not about the type of food Peter was supposed to eat, but who the gospel was to be preached to. Peter finally got the correct interpretation:

> God has shown me that I should not call any man unholy or unclean (Acts 10:28).

Inaccurate Words

Any of us who have been around prophetic ministry can understand why Paul had to say the following:

> *Do not quench the Spirit; do not despise prophetic utterances. But examine everything carefully; hold fast to that which is good (1 Thessalonians 5:19-21).*

If Paul would bring up the subject that we should not despise prophecy, that means that we may want to at times. Many churches, in response to poor and abusive prophetic ministry, have eliminated the gifts of the Holy Spirit from their services. Their fear of "false prophets" has quenched the gift of prophecy within the church.

How do we handle incorrect prophecy?

It is important to remember that we are all in training and prophetic people can make a mistake without being false prophets. We have to not judge ones who just "miss it" so much as they could be doing the best they can for where they are in their faith.

Even the apostles and prophets in the Bible gave prophesies that were not entirely accurate. Agabus the prophet prophesied that Paul would be bound by the Jews in Jerusalem and handed over to the Gentiles:

> *As we were staying there for some days, a prophet named Agabus came down from Judea. And coming to us, he took Paul's belt and bound his own feet and hands, and said, "This is what the Holy Spirit says: 'In this way the Jews at Jerusalem will bind the man who owns this belt and deliver him into the hands of the Gentiles'" (Acts 21:10-11).*

What actually happened was that the Roman soldiers (Gentiles) rescued Paul from the Jews and it was the soldiers who bound Paul, not the Jews:

> *While they were seeking to kill him, a report came up to the commander of the Roman cohort that all Jerusalem was in confusion. At once he took along some soldiers and centurions and ran down to them; and when they saw the commander and the soldiers, they stopped beating Paul. Then the commander came up and took hold of him, and ordered him to be bound with two chains; and he began asking who he was and what he had done (Acts 21:31-33).*

Another example is found when Paul gave a word to the crew of a ship he was about to sail on:

> *Paul began to admonish them, and said to them, "Men, I perceive that the voyage will certainly be with damage and great loss, not only of the cargo and the ship, but also of our lives" (Acts 27:9-10).*

Paul later corrected himself after an encounter with an angel, only the ship would be lost, but the crew would be saved. Paul did not have it right the first time!

> *...then Paul stood up in their midst and said, "Men, you ought to have followed my advice and not to have set sail from Crete and incurred this damage and loss. Yet now I urge you to keep up your courage, for there will be no loss of life among you, but only of the ship. For this very night an angel of the God to whom I belong and whom I serve stood before me, saying, 'Do not be afraid, Paul; you must stand before Caesar; and behold, God has granted you all those who are sailing with you'" (Acts 27:21-25).*

Receiving Negative Words

What do you do with a negative word?

A negative word that is given by an immature prophet can release that reality in your life. A correct word given in the wrong spirit can cause damage. The Lord will also give us words of warning and correction.

Moses received a negative word concerning the sin of the people:

> The Lord spoke further to me, saying, "I have seen this people, and indeed, it is a stubborn people. Let Me alone, that I may destroy them and blot out their name from under heaven; and I will make of you a nation mightier and greater than they" (Deuteronomy 9:13-14).

Moses interceded for 40 days and changed the circumstances. Remember, your prayers and intercession are powerful!

> So I fell down before the Lord the forty days and nights, which I did because the Lord had said He would destroy you. I prayed to the Lord and said, "O Lord God, do not destroy Your people, even Your inheritance, whom You have redeemed through Your greatness, whom You have brought out of Egypt with a mighty hand" (Deuteronomy 9:25-26).

Another example of prayer changing a prophetic word is the prophetic word given to Hezekiah from the prophet Isaiah concerning Hezekiah's illness:

> In those days Hezekiah became mortally ill. And Isaiah the prophet, the son of Amoz, came to him and said to him, "Thus says the Lord, 'Set your house in order, for you shall die and not live'" (2 Kings 20:1).

The power of Hezekiah's prayer is evident when the Lord added 15 years to his life as a result of those prayers:

> Then he turned his face to the wall and prayed to the Lord, saying, "Remember now, O Lord, I beseech You, how I have walked before You in truth and with a whole heart and have done what is good in Your sight." And Hezekiah wept bitterly. Before Isaiah had gone out of the middle court, the word of the Lord came to him, saying, "Return and say to Hezekiah the leader of My people, 'Thus says the Lord, the

God of your father David, "I have heard your prayer, I have seen your tears; behold, I will heal you. On the third day you shall go up to the house of the Lord. I will add fifteen years to your life"' (2 Kings 20:2-6).

False Prophets

The Bible warns of false prophets many times, especially in these "last days."

Beware of the false prophets, who come to you in sheep's clothing, but inwardly are ravenous wolves. You will know them by their fruits (Matthew 7:15-16).

A false prophet is not someone who gives a bad or inaccurate word, but someone who prophesies from a wrong spirit or an evil heart. A false prophet is able to prophecy accurately from a demonic spirit. Paul encountered such a person in the following verses. The entire prophecy that was given was correct. Demons can operate accurately in the Word of Knowledge because they can see and hear. Demons cannot prophesy the future; if they could, the devil would never have put into the hearts of the people to crucify Jesus!

It happened that as we were going to the place of prayer, a slave-girl having a spirit of divination met us, who were bringing her masters much profit by fortune-telling. Following after Paul and us, she kept crying out, saying, "These men are bond-servants of the Most High God, who are proclaiming to you the way of salvation." She continued doing this for many days. But Paul was greatly annoyed, and turned and said to the spirit, "I command you in the name of Jesus Christ to come out of her!" And it came out at that very moment (Acts 16:16- 18).

Characteristics of False Prophets (Acts 16:16-18):

- They operate from a spirit of divination.
- They knowingly deceive people.
- They knowingly use signs and wonders to deceive people. (Mark 13:22)
- They use flattery, seduction and manipulation (Jezebel spirit).

Another type of false prophet is one who started out right, but allowed compromise and sin into their lives and has fallen away from God. They can still operate in the prophetic gift:

> ...for the gifts and the calling of God are irrevocable (Romans 11:29).

Characteristics of False Prophets – Issues of the Heart:

- They have a wounded heart.
- They lose accountability to the scripture and place themselves above the Word of God.
- Their heart is closed to new revelation and unwilling to allow people to test their prophecy.
- They seek to promote themselves and their own personal agendas.
- They prophesy for personal gain, either wealth or influence. They prophesy what people want to hear for personal gain.
- Draw people to themselves instead of Jesus.
- We will know them by their fruit, they do not walk in the Fruits of the Spirit which are love, joy, peace, patience, kindness, goodness, faithfulness, gentleness and self-control. A true prophet will demonstrate the character of the Holy Spirit.

The Prophetic Word Often Comes as a Seed

> Hear then the parable of the sower. When anyone hears the word of the kingdom and does not understand it, the

evil one comes and snatches away what has been sown in his heart. This is the one on whom seed was sown beside the road. The one on whom seed was sown on the rocky places, this is the man who hears the word and immediately receives it with joy; yet he has no firm root in himself, but is only temporary, and when affliction or persecution arises because of the word, immediately he falls away. And the one on whom seed was sown among the thorns, this is the man who hears the word, and the worry of the world and the deceitfulness of wealth choke the word, and it becomes unfruitful. And the one on whom seed was sown on the good soil, this is the man who hears the word and understands it; who indeed bears fruit and brings forth, some a hundredfold, some sixty, and some thirty (Matthew 13:18-23).

<u>Seeds Beside the Road</u> – Speaks of when we do not take time to properly receive, meditate and test the word to understand it for our lives.

<u>Seeds Sown on Rocky Places</u> – Speaks of when we allow the attacks by the enemy which are meant to stop the release of God's plans and purposes to lives to be successful.

<u>Seeds Sown Among the Thorns</u> - Speaks of when we allow the temptations and worries of this world to choke out our pursuit of God's purposes for our lives.

<u>Seeds Sown on Good Soil</u> – Speaks of when God's plan and purposes in our life are allowed to grow into maturity and become fruitful.

Seeds sown are the prophetic words spoken from the heart of God and are the "Word of the Kingdom" as described in v.18. Words from the Lord are precious and God does use people to deliver those words to us. Just because they are spoken to us from someone else, even a friend, does not make them less important than if an angel or the Lord Himself spoke them to us.

We should never be so busy that we just "put the word on the shelf" and move on without processing what the Lord is saying.

We should journal our prophetic words and take time to go back and read them, asking the Holy Spirit to give us revelation and understanding. We first allow our true prophetic words to be seeds within our heart. After we receive the word, we must learn to water the word.

Birthing Prophetic Seeds in the Glory

We must play our part in order to have prophecy come to pass. It is vital to realize that even accurate prophecies about the future do not usually come to pass automatically. We have to do something in order for them to be fulfilled.

In the beginning, God created the heavens and the earth. The earth was formless and void, and darkness was over the surface of the deep, and the Spirit of God was moving over the surface of the waters. Then God said, "Let there be light," and there was light (Genesis 1:1-3).

During creation there were two powerful forces present:

First, was the Spirit of God which was hovering or moving over the surface of the waters. The Spirit of God is the very essence of God, the presence of God or the glory of God.

The second powerful force present during creation was "Then God said," or the Word of God. These two powerful forces, The presence or glory of God and the Word of God when combined together have creative power.

As we worship, whether it is in our corporate or individual time, often the presence of God, or His glory will manifest in our midst. The prophetic promises spoken over our lives are the Word of God. Take the words that are burning within your heart and prophesy them into the Glory. As you do this, you are Partnering with the same two powerful forces that were present during creation.

Activation

Take some time to pray for your city with worship music playing to set the atmosphere.

Write down what the Lord is saying about your city.

Gather as a group and declare them over your city as if it were a person standing in front of you. Take turns speaking prophetic blessings over your city and then write them down so that you can watch them come to pass.

Prophetic Challenge

Remember and review previous prophetic words that have been given to you. Write them in your journal if you have not done so yet. Begin to mediate and pray over these words. Ask the Lord which ones you should begin to birth now. Birth those words in the glory!

NOTES

A Field Guide to Prophetic Ministry

DREAMS

In a dream, in a vision of the night, when deep sleep falls upon men, while slumbering on their beds, then He opens the ears of men, and seals their instruction (Job 33:15-16).

1. Our ears are open. (Job: 33:16)
2. Our minds are quieted.
3. Our spirits never sleep. (Psalm 121:4)
4. Our analytical skepticism is gone.
5. To hide mystery for us to seek it out. (Proverbs 25:2)

Jim Goll says in his book *Dream Language*, "Visions reveal God's nature while dreams often give us direction or reveal some part of God's plan."

The Purpose of Dreams

- It leads to the Heart of the Father- dreams should draw us closer to the Lord as we journal and spend time prayerfully pondering the meaning. When we are asleep, we are free from distractions and our barriers are down. The Lord can speak directly to us through dreams.
- It awakens our walk with Him.
- It imparts intercessory burdens.
- It launches you into ministry.
- It brings healing.

Hear now my words: If there is a prophet among you, I, the Lord, shall make Myself known to him in a vision. I shall speak with him in a dream" (Numbers 12:6).

God speaks to His people in a dream and will make Himself known in a vision. He uses both visions and dreams to draw us to His purposes.

Examples of those God has Communicated to in Dreams:

<u>God warned ungodly kings and rulers through dreams:</u>

But God came to Abimelech in a dream by night, and said to him, "Indeed you are a dead man because of the woman whom you have taken, for she is a man's wife" (Genesis 20:3).

And God said to him in a dream, "Yes, I know that you did this in the integrity of your heart. God also withheld you from sinning against Me; therefore I did not let you touch her" (Genesis 20:6).

<u>God gave Jacob the ability to get wealth in his dream:</u>

And it happened, at the time when the flocks conceived, that I lifted my eyes and saw in a dream, and behold, the rams which leaped upon the flocks were streaked, speckled, and gray-spotted. Then the Angel of God spoke to me in a dream, saying, "Jacob." And I said, "Here I am." And He said, "Lift your eyes now and see, all the rams which leap on the flocks are streaked, speckled, and gray-spotted; for I have seen all that Laban is doing to you. I am the God of Bethel, where you anointed the pillar and where you made a vow to Me. Now arise, get out of this land, and return to the land of your family" (Genesis 31:10-13).

<u>God warned Laban not to do any harm to Jacob in a dream:</u>

But God had come to Laban the Syrian in a dream by night, and said to him, "Be careful that you speak to Jacob neither good nor bad" (Genesis 31:24).

The Lord appeared to Solomon in a dream and imparted wisdom and an understanding heart:

At Gibeon the Lord appeared to Solomon in a dream by night; and God said, "Ask! What shall I give you?" (1 Kings 3:5).

In verses 9-15 of this same chapter, Solomon asks God to give him an understanding heart (hearing ear) to judge God's people and that he would discern between good and evil. God granted this to Solomon as well as, riches and honor, which he did not ask for. God also gave him a long life. When Solomon woke up, he realized it had been a dream.

The birth of Jesus was orchestrated and directed through dreams and visions. Matthew 1:18-25 tells of when Joseph was deciding what to do about Mary, his fiancée. The scripture states that an angel of the Lord appeared to him in a dream saying, "Joseph, son of David, do not be afraid to take to you Mary your wife, for that which is conceived in her is of the Holy Spirit."

Also, the wise men and Joseph were divinely warned in a dream:

And having been warned by God in a dream not to return to Herod, the magi left for their own country by another way. Now when they had gone, behold, an angel of the Lord appeared to Joseph in a dream and said, "Get up! Take the Child and His mother and flee to Egypt, and remain there until I tell you; for Herod is going to search for the Child to destroy Him" (Matthew 2:12-13).

Types of Dreams

A Simple Message Dream - no need for interpretation. These dreams are direct and to the point and self-interpreted.

*Example: Matthew 1-2 - Joseph's dream concerning Mary and Herod.

The Simple Symbolic Dream- Dreams can be filled with symbols. The symbolism is clear enough that the dreamer and others can understand it without complicated interpretation.

*Example: Joseph's dream in Genesis 37.

The Complex Symbolic Dream- this type of dream needs interpretive skill from someone who has the ability in the gift of interpretation or from someone who knows how to seek God to find revelation.

*Example: Read Daniel 2, 4 and 8.

Recording and Interpreting Your Dreams:

1. Name, date and title your dream, record your waking time. Daniel 7:1 - Daniel had a dream and visions in his head while on his bed. Then he wrote down the dream, telling the main facts.
2. Write or draw your dream out in bullet point, diagram, outline or paragraph form.
3. Record the main facts and eliminate the unnecessary details
4. Ask the Holy Spirit for insight and understanding of the dream.
5. Does the dream symbol appear in the Bible? Search it out in the Word. Dreams from the Lord will never go against His word. (Prov. 25:2)
6. Ask questions about what you saw in your dream What did you sense and feel from the dream? Was it a good or evil presence, fear, love, concern, hopelessness, disappointment? What was the primary emotion? What are the colors? Is everything in black and white or in color? (Zechariah 4)

7. Look for the theme or essence the dream is communicating to you. Relate the dreams to your circumstances and spheres of influence. Consecutive dreams often have the same or similar meaning. (Gen.41:1-7, 25-31). God will speak the same message more than once.
8. Keeping it simple is better than trying to complicate the dream.
9. Visualize the dream as you recall or rehearse the main symbols in the scenes of the dream.

When understanding and interpreting dreams, remember that our Heavenly Father has given us a Helper and will reveal truth to us. All we have to do is ask.

But the Helper, the Holy Spirit, whom the Father will send in My name, He will teach you all things, and bring to your remembrance all that I said to you (John 14:26).

But when He, the Spirit of truth, comes, He will guide you into all the truth; for He will not speak on His own initiative, but whatever He hears, He will speak; and He will disclose to you what is to come. He will glorify Me, for He will take of Mine and will disclose it to you. All things that the Father has are Mine; therefore I said that He takes of Mine and will disclose it to you (1 John 16:13-15).

But if any of you lacks wisdom, let him ask of God, who gives to all generously and without reproach, and it will be given to him. But he must ask in faith without any doubting, for the one who doubts is like the surf of the sea, driven and tossed by the wind. For that man ought not to expect that he will receive anything from the Lord, being a double-minded man, unstable in all his ways (James 1:5-8).

Creating a Culture for Revelation

The following was taken from *Dream Language* by Jim Goll:

1. Pull out your spiritual antenna- we have to be tuned in and ready to receive God's transmissions. Get ready and expect to receive.
2. The Power of the Blood – "And not through the blood of goats and calves, but through His own blood, He entered the holy place once for all, having obtained eternal redemption" (Hebrews 9:12).
3. Pray in the Spirit - "But you, beloved, build yourselves up on you most holy faith, praying in the Holy Spirit" (Jude 20). Praying in the Spirit refreshes us, stirs our faith, and creates an atmosphere where God's mysteries are spoken and revealed.
4. Meditate on God's Word - "This book of the law shall not depart from your mouth, but you shall meditate on it day and night, so that you may be careful to do according to all that is written in it; for then you will make your way prosperous, and then you will have success" (Joshua 1:8).
5. Worship and sing praises- 2 Chronicles 20:18-22 talks about the worshippers going ahead of the army and defeating the enemy by their praise.

The Drain to Dreaming

1. Church Culture and Worldview - Wrong traditions and worldview have stolen the relevance of dreaming. There has been no place for dreams in materialistic and logical scientism. We have moved away from our Hebraic foundation and shifted into a Greek mindset. This philosophy produces an analytical mindset.

2. Are you at rest or are you striving? - "For thus the Lord God, the Holy One of Israel, has said, 'In repentance and

rest you will be saved, in quietness and trust is your strength'" (Isaiah 30:15).

3. Is your receptor clean? - "Be renewed in the spirit of your mind, and put on the new self, which in the likeness of God has been created in righteousness and holiness of the truth. Therefore, laying aside falsehood, speak truth each one of you with his neighbor, for we are members of one another. Be angry, and yet do not sin, do not let the sun go down on your anger, and do not give the devil an opportunity" (Ephesians 4:23-27).

- Worry- Psalm 37:8
- Anger- Ephesians 4:26
- Lust- Romans 13:10-14
- Bitterness- Hebrews 12:15

Our spirit must be able to receive. We must be careful what we watch and listen to. We must not give place to the devil. We must not grieve the Holy Spirit.

4. Our Routine - Inconsistent schedules can hinder the flow and retention of revelation. A lot of times this is not our fault, it's just due to the demands of life. Ask the Lord for His grace and to help you work out your schedule and even to alter it, if needed. Set apart times for receiving from the Lord. Sacrifice releases power. Fasting can be used to soften our heart and to put us in a position for heavenly downloads.

5. To Whom Much is Given? - "For whoever has, to him more shall be given, and he will have an abundance; but whoever does not have, even what he has shall be taken away from him. Therefore, I speak to them in parables; because while seeing they do not see, and while hearing they do not hear, nor do they understand. In their hearing, but will not understand; you will keep on seeing, but will not perceive; for the heart of this people has become dull with their ears they scarcely hear, and they have closed their eyes, otherwise they would see with their eyes, hear

with their ears, and understand with their heart and return, and I would heal them" (Matthew 13:12-16).

If we do not pay attention to what we have already received, the Holy Spirit is not obligated to give us more. Faithfulness brings reward!

6. Integrity is a Major Issue - Both the Holy Spirit and people are drawn to integrity. Tomorrow's call does not give you authority today. There is a learning process of being called, trained, and commissioned. Don't distort the meaning of a dream out of your insecurity. Don't say more than God says or more than God said to say. Learn to pray and hold- wait for more revelation before you speak.

Other things that will hinder our dreams could be:

1. Distraction - The scripture says to set our minds on things above and not on earthly things. We need to set aside time to receive revelation away from distractions- cell phone, computer, TV, books, magazines, friends, and family.

2. Disinformation - What does God have to say in His Word? God still speaks to us today. Too often, as Christians, we are looking to institutions, denominations and uniformed people to get our theology rather than basing it on the Word of God. Wrong information and lack of information is a culture that allows the doubts of darkness to breed and remain. Hosea 4:6 says, "My people are destroyed for lack of knowledge."

3. Disbelief - Many can't and will not hear the voice of the Holy Spirit in their lives because they do not believe God wants to speak to them. Disbelief can filter out God's love, care, revelation and at times His empowering. Remember that we serve an all-powerful, all-knowing God who has spoken, is speaking and will continue to speak to His people. The scripture in Mark 9:23 states, "I do believe, help my unbelief!"

Things to Remember in Keeping Interpretation Simple

- Most of all, dreams should be interpreted on a personal basis first. (John 10:3)
- Most dreams should not be taken literally. They need to be interpreted. (Daniel 1:17)
- God will use familiar terms you know. (Matthew 4:19)
- Ponder on the dream or revelation and ask the Holy Spirit for insight. (Daniel 7:8)
- Ask the Holy Spirit what the certain thought, word, or issue is in the revelation. Reduce the dream to its simplest form. What is the main thought? What object or thought occurs most often?
- Search it out in the Word. Dreams from the Lord will never go against His word. (Proverbs 25:2)
- What did you sense and feel from the dream? Was it a good or evil presence, fear, love, concern, hopelessness, disappointment? What was the primary emotion?
- Relate the dreams to your circumstances and spheres of influence.
- Consecutive dreams often have the same or similar meaning.
- What are the colors?
- Interpretations can be three levels:
    - Personal
    - Church congregation, city church, church in a nation, global body of Christ
    - National and international - these can be governmental in nature.
- More than one interpretation can come from one dream. Just like in scripture, there is a historical context as well as the personal, present implication. In dreams, it might be a general word for the church with specific applications for yourself.
- Some dreams may only be understood in the future. They unfold over time. Details will make sense down the road.

- Write down the summary, date it, where you were, the time, if you woke up from it, the main emotions and a possible interpretation in a journal.
- The key to proper interpretation is to question, question, and question. (See Zechariah 4)

Activation

Split up into groups of 3 or 4 and tell of a dream you had recently. Using some of the dream symbols (starting on page 97) and prayer try to interpret the dream.

Prophetic Challenge

Prepare yourself for dreams by surrendering to the Holy Spirit before you go to sleep. Ask the Lord to speak to you in your sleep. When you awake, write down any dreams you have and begin to seek the Lord for the interpretation.

NOTES

COMMON SYMBOLS & INTERPRETATION

(This list is not made to be all encompassing. As with anything in the Christian walk, pray, and seek wise counsel as to what interpretations may or may not be.)

Colors

- Amber – contamination, holiness, idolatry, purity
- Black - stability, death
- Blue – anxiety, depression, revelation, communion, truth, peace
- Brown- Pastor, humanism, compassion, order, earth
- Cyan (light blue) - Fasting, will
- Gold- contamination, holiness, purity, wealth, prosperity, wisdom
- Gray – weak, sorrow, security, maturity
- Faded Colors-weakens meaning of color
- Green- pride, envy, conscience, life, nature, fertility
- Magenta- emotion, giving
- Orange- perseverance, stubbornness, vitality
- Pink-love, beauty
- Purple-authority, royalty, false authority, intercession
- Red- anointing, praying, anger, war, wisdom, courage, vitality, action
- Silver-redemption
- Yellow-fear, hope, mind, joy, happiness
- White-purity, cleanliness

Numbers

1- God, unity

2- Division, judgment, multiplication, split, difference, opposition

3- Godhead or triune God, complete

4- God's creative works

5- Grace, redemption

6- Man

7- Completion, perfection

8- New beginnings, teacher

9- Evangelist, judgment

10- Journey, pastor, wilderness

11- Prophet, revelation, transition

12- Apostle, government

13- Rebellion

14- Double anointing

15- Mercy, pardon, reprieve

16- Established beginnings

17- Election or elect

18- Established blessing

24- Elders around the throne

25- Begin ministry training

30- Begin ministry

40- Completed rule, generation

50- Freedom, jubilee

111- My beloved Son

120- End of flesh

153- Kingdom multiplication

555- Triple grace

666- Full lawlessness

888- Resurrection

1500- Authority, light, power

Animals

- Alligator- bossy spirit, great influencer, big mouth
- Ants- irritation, unwanted guests
- Armadillo- nuisance, harasser, destroyer
- Bat- satanic torment
- Bear- demonic force, hungry for something you have
- Bee- higher demonic power, but less lethal
- Birds- kingdom of heaven
- Cat- a watching demonic spirit, independent thinker
- Chicken- being chicken
- Cobra- spirit of control and manipulation
- Cow- slow laborious change
- Crab- hard shell, not easy to approach

- Crocodile- big mouth, something that can drag you down, vicious verbal attack
- Dog- friend
- Donkey- stubborn
- Dragon- satan or his plans
- Duck- false or quack as in a charlatan
- Eagles- prophetic
- Elephant- demonic force designed to attack your mind, humanism
- Frog- counterfeit of conscience, lust, sexual spirit
- Hamster- running around in circles
- Hippopotamus- big mouth, bossy spirit, great influencer
- Hornet- higher demonic power, less lethal
- Horse- power, sometimes major or for movement of God
- Ladybugs- eat the harassers
- Lion- intimidation, power
- Lion attacking you- God coming against you
- Lizard- lying (long tale)
- Ox- slow laborious change
- Panther (black) - high level of witchcraft
- Pigs- carriers of demons
- Rabbit- sexual torment
- Rams- satanic occult
- Rat- garbage (sin)
- Ravens-soul
- Rhinoceros- critical and harsh
- Scorpion- someone wanting to do you in, witchcraft
- Sharks- vicious or malicious activity by people you know
- Snake- backbiting, divination, false accusations, false prophecies, gossip, long tales, slander
- Spider- demonic attack, occult
- Spider web- demonic network
- Tigers- soul power
- Zebra- a horse that looks righteous, but has soulish issues

Miscellaneous

- Airplane-church, large corporation
- Amphitheater- something is going to be magnified
- Angel- good will toward men, messenger
- Ann-grace
- Arm- strength
- Armored car- major protection
- Atrium- glass indicates vision
- Attic- past history issues, storing things God has given you that get dusty
- Autograph- prominence or fame
- Back porch- history
- Bald head- lacking wisdom
- Ball gown- prepared for something that requires elegance
- Banner- victory
- Basement- hidden or unseen
- Bathroom-cleansing
- Bed-intimacy
- Bent knees- prayer
- Bike- individual ministry or calling
- Books-knowledge, preparation time
- Braking car- warning to slow down
- Breasts- ability to nurse young
- Bright from a light-from God
- Brothers- the body of Christ
- Buckler- protection
- Bus- church or ministry
- Cafeteria-spiritual food
- Candle- impact, influence
- Car- job or vocation, personal ministry, small church, small ministry
- Car repair- minister/ministry healing
- Chariot- major encounter, life destiny
- Children- next generation
- City- God's inner city, inner city work
- Clouds, dark- from the enemy
- Clouds, light- from God
- Coat- mantle

- Columns- foundations people put trust in
- Controlled flying- spiritual maturity increasing
- Convertible- open heaven
- Cracked basement walls- problems in the foundation
- Crops-different lengths of time
- Crossing street- changing perspective, changing place of operation.
- Cultural clothes- call to nation
- Dart- piercing, penetrating or painful experience
- Dead body- being dead in the gifts
- Dining room- eating spiritual food
- Door- walking through something
- Double number- double of what the number means
- Dreadlocks- rebellion
- Driving in reverse- not going the direction you should be with the anointing you have
- Dusty- neglected, lack of use
- Eating- eating spiritual food
- Eighteen wheeler- blessing of ministry, judgment of ministry
- Elevator- change in anointing: up=increase, down=decrease
- Evening gown-what you are called to requires elegance
- Eyetooth- vision or revelation
- Face, dark- demonic
- Face, lightened- angelic
- Family pictures- family historical issues
- Farm- feeding
- Fast- easy
- Feathers-comfort, confusion, covering
- Fingernails- weapons
- Fingers- ability to relate, direction, intertwine
- Fire, roaring- God devouring His enemy
- Flamingo- instruments that carry out the purposes of God
- Flash- revelation or insight
- Flowers- fragrance
- Flying- spiritual advancement

- Forehead- peace of mind
- Former place- season you are currently in or coming to
- Fred Flintstone car- human effort
- Freezer- Storing spiritual food for future time
- Front porch- vision
- Garden- place of growth or intimacy, place of love/romance as in Song of Solomon
- Gas station- power
- Gas station, old- old power
- Gun- spiritual authority either good or bad
- Gymnasium- great discipline
- Hair- wisdom
- Hair, long- growing wisdom
- Hair, short- cut off wisdom
- Hand- direction
- Head- mind, intellect
- Hills- elevation
- Hole in clothes- worn out or too old
- Hospital- healing
- Hotel- people come, get touched and move on
- House- your church, family, your life
- House, live in someone else's- similar anointing
- Immobilization of body parts- demonic hindrances to what you are doing in the Lord
- Incisor teeth- ability to decide
- Index finger- prophetic
- Jeans- completing or walking out what you are called to do
- Jet- church or large corporation
- Kiss- humility
- Kitchen- preparing spiritual food
- Knee- humility
- Knife- holding a knife- protection, verbal responses such as sharp tongue
- Lava- enemy, vicious slow attack against people of God
- Left- gifts that you were born with
- Left side- born with
- Limousine- call of God

- Lying on stomach- humble
- Machine guns- high power weapons
- Mall- church, egotism or selfishness
- Mickey Mouse car- animated, colorful and entertaining, ideological, theoretical
- Mobile Home- going to be changing homes, temporary condition
- Money- favor
- Money, lost- loss of favor
- Mountain- God's presence, the Lord
- Nakedness- nothing hidden, vulnerable, without guile
- Names in scripture- to prophesy what's about to happen to a people
- Neck- willingness, stubborn
- Nightgown- darkness
- Nose- discernment
- Ocean- church, masses of people
- Ocean liner- church that is mission minded, large movement
- Office- calling and gifts
- Top of head- indicates position and rank
- Outer space- insight into the cosmos
- Pants- completing or walking out what you are called to do
- Parked car- ministry on the sideline
- Parking lots- short term levels
- Picture frames, gold- framed by God for a precious purpose
- Pornography- deterioration, soulish desires, you came in contact with this spirit
- Private jet- instructions, you and God alone
- Property- responsibility
- Prophet- represents a prophetic word

For more reading and to study this subject further:

Dream Interpretation Guidelines-Christian Dream Symbols by Brenda McDonald

Dream Language by Jim Goll

Dream Encounters by Barbie Breathitt

Dreams-Divinity Code, The Key to Decoding your Dreams and Visions by Adrian Beale and Adam F. Thompson

Website: www.streamsministries.com (John Paul Jackson)

GROWING IN THE PROPHETIC

And Jesus kept increasing in wisdom and stature, and in favor with God and men (Luke 2:52).

A question that is frequently asked is, "How does one grow in prophetic ministry?" It is not wrong to ask for spiritual gifts as the Word tells us to eagerly desire them. The key is to "grow up in all aspects into Him who is the head, even Christ" (Ephesians 4:15). Prophecy and Words of Knowledge will flow naturally as we come to intimately know Jesus, who is the "Word."

There are Three Types of Prophetic Anointing:

1. Operating in the Spirit of Prophecy – The Spirit of Prophecy is often a beginner's stage in the prophetic. Mark Virkler defines it as, "Not being able to personally capture the prophetic flow unless you have been led into it by another." A Spirit of Prophecy is often a corporate anointing of the Holy Spirit, which enables men, and women who do not operate in the Gift of Prophecy or the Office of the Prophet to speak forth under the inspiration of God. Such anointing is usually released in meetings where there is a powerful presence of the Lord and almost anyone could pick up on the mind of the Lord and prophesy. People find it easier to receive visions, prophesy of edification, exhortation and comfort, which always lead people to Jesus. This is the testimony of Jesus.

And he said to me, "These are true words of God." Then I fell at his feet to worship him. But he said to me, "Do not do that; I am a fellow servant of yours and your brethren who hold the testimony of Jesus; worship God. For the testimony of Jesus is the spirit of prophecy" (Rev 19:9-10).

2. Operating in the Gift of Prophecy – The Gift of Prophecy – The Gift of Prophecy is when a person has personally developed to be able to flow in the prophetic even when the Spirit of Prophecy is not present. This person has learned how to stand still before God, even in a group of people and "stir up the gift" that is within them. Growing in the operation of the Gift of Prophecy is available to all who seek it. Second Timothy 1:6 indicates this gift can be imparted through the laying on of hands.

But to each one is given the manifestation of the Spirit for the common good. For to one is given the word of wisdom through the Spirit, and to another the word of knowledge according to the same Spirit; to another faith by the same Spirit, and to another gifts of healing by the one Spirit, and to another the effecting of miracles, and to another prophecy, and to another the distinguishing of spirits, to another various kinds of tongues, and to another the interpretation of tongues (1 Corinthians 12:7-10).

3. Operating in the Office of the Prophet – The Office of the Prophet is basically developed when leaders in the Body of Christ as having a mature prophetic ministry recognize you. In Luke 2:32 Jesus grew "in favor" with God and men. Paul said in Romans 11:13, "I am an apostle of Gentiles," indicating that he was an apostle to the Gentiles because he was received as such, but not to the Jews. A person who operates in the Office of a Prophet will often operate in the prophetic realm of foretelling and confirmation of ministries within the Body of Christ. God sets people into this office.

The Office of the Prophet is designed to function in a higher realm of ministry than the Gift of Prophecy. The

Office of the Prophet is part of the five-fold ministry gifts intended to build up, encourage, and comfort the Church, but also to give guidance, instruction and can bring correction.

And He gave some as apostles, and some as prophets, and some as evangelists, and some as pastors and teachers, for the equipping of the saints for the work of service, to the building up of the body of Christ (Ephesians 4:11-12).

Before I formed you in the womb I knew you, And before you were born I consecrated you; I have appointed you a prophet to the nations" (Jeremiah 1:5).

Knowing God – God is always speaking, but we are not always listening. The mark of intimacy is hearing His voice. Hearing the voice of God is part of the joy of a relationship with Him. There are secrets that are reserved only for the friends of God who pursue Him in intimacy. The purpose of our pursuit is not just hearing His voice, but becoming a "friend of God." As we begin to walk in this type of relationship we will see the Kingdom of God manifested. Make the presence of the Lord your treasure!

No longer do I call you slaves, for the slave does not know what his master is doing; but I have called you friends, for all things that I have heard from My Father I have made known to you. You did not choose Me but I chose you, and appointed you that you would go and bear fruit, and that your fruit would remain, so that whatever you ask of the Father in My name He may give to you (John 15:15-16).

Thus the Lord used to speak to Moses face to face, just as a man speaks to his friend (Exodus 33:11).

The secret of the Lord (friendship of the Lord) is for those who fear Him, And He will make them know His covenant (Psalm 25:14).

...but you have received a spirit of adoption as sons by which we cry out, "Abba! Father!" The Spirit Himself testifies with our spirit that we are children of God, and if children, heirs also, heirs of God and fellow heirs with Christ (Romans 8:15-17).

<u>Consecration</u> – As we consecrate ourselves we allow ourselves to be drawn closer into the presence of God. We remove obstacles that prevent us from hearing His voice. Invite the Holy Spirit to convict you of any unconfessed sins. Guard your "eye gate" and "ear gate" from things that will defile and vex your soul. Be filled with the Word and with the Holy Spirit.

Position yourself to hear His voice by:

- Worship
- Mediation and Prayer
- Develop a continual fellowship with the Holy Spirit
- Listening

Then Joshua said to the people, "Consecrate yourselves, for tomorrow the Lord will do wonders among you" (Joshua 3:5).

And do not be conformed to this world, but be transformed by the renewing of your mind, so that you may prove what the will of God is, that which is good and acceptable and perfect (Romans 12:2).

But the fruit of the Spirit is love, joy, peace, patience, kindness, goodness, faithfulness, gentleness, self-control; against such things there is no law. Now those who belong to Christ Jesus have crucified the flesh with its passions and desires (Galatians 5:22-24).

Now for this very reason also, applying all diligence, in your faith supply moral excellence, and in your moral excellence, knowledge, and in your knowledge, self-control, and in your self-control, perseverance, and in your perseverance, godliness, and in your godliness, brotherly kindness, and in your brotherly kindness, love. For if these qualities are yours and are increasing, they render you neither useless nor unfruitful in the true knowledge of our Lord Jesus Christ. For he who lacks these qualities is blind or short-sighted, having forgotten his purification from his former sins (2 Peter 1:5-9).

Appointed – From 2000 to 2010 Reinhard Bonnke's ministry had about 60 million decisions for Christ. Reinhard thanked God one day for choosing him to bring in the mighty harvest of souls. The Lord told Reinhard that he was not His first choice for this job. God had asked others before Reinhard, but they would not respond to His call. God calls many to become His friends, to draw near and to hear His voice. Sadly, few are willing to die to themselves and say "YES."

God appoints those who say "YES!"

For many are called, but few are chosen (Matthew 22:14).

God is looking for people that will listen for His voice!

For the eyes of the Lord move to and fro throughout the earth that He may strongly support those whose heart is completely His (2 Chronicles 16:9).

To be a prophet is a calling. To minister in prophecy is a gift.

"When a person ministers in the gift of prophecy, the gift is the ability to prophesy. The words themselves are the gift. When a person is a prophet, they themselves are the gift. The book of Ephesians says, "Christ gave gifts to men." The gifts that He gave are other men. A prophet is a gift to the church." – Kris Vallotton

Present Prophecy with Humility, Teach-ability and Patience

Humility – desire to not bring glory to yourself. We are part of a nameless, faceless generation that always directs glory to Jesus. Our goal is to be known in heaven, not upon the earth.

He who has the bride is the bridegroom; but the friend of the bridegroom, who stands and hears Him, rejoices greatly because of the bridegroom's voice. So this joy of mine has been made full. He must increase, but I must decrease (John 3:29-30).

Teach-ability – We recognize that we "see in part" and need the rest of the Body of Christ. We are willing to receive instruction from others in administering revelation.

Let two or three prophets speak, and let the others pass judgment (1 Corinthians 14:29).

Patience – We must be willing to be patient after we prophecy for the word to come to pass in God's timing.

BY THE MOUTH OF TWO OR THREE WITNESSES EVERY FACT MAY BE CONFIRMED (Matthew 18:16).

A Prophet's Reward

He who receives a prophet in the name of a prophet shall receive a prophet's reward (Matthew 10:41).

Receiving a prophet is more than just listening to the word that is given. Receiving involves placing a value on the prophetic word and making room for that word in your life. The reward comes as we properly receive the prophetic word and we receive the anointing to see that word manifest.

The reward of a Prophet is the ability to see and to hear spiritually.

But what is the reward for the prophet giving the word?

Evangelists often have instant reward when they give an altar call to see sinners come forward to receive Jesus. A person giving a prophetic word may not always see that word come to pass. Our reward must not be in the fruits of the word that we give. Our reward must be based upon that we are the ones God speaks to, we are friends of God who receive revelation. Our reward must always be His presence.

Practicing the Gift of Prophecy

Do not neglect the spiritual gift within you, which was bestowed on you through prophetic utterance with the laying on of hands by the presbytery. Take pains with these things; be absorbed in them, so that your progress will be evident to all (1 Timothy 4:14-16).

Many people misunderstand the definition of practicing the gifts of the Holy Spirit. When Jesus sent the Holy Spirit to the church in Acts Chapter 2, He released to us the same potential of anointing, power and giftings that He walked in. We do not practice so that the Holy Spirit can improve His gifts, but rather we practice to improve our ability to flow with what the Holy Spirit is doing.

Paul is telling Timothy to minister in the spiritual gifts beyond his comfort zone. If we only minister where we feel comfortable at, we will never grow in those gifts. Classrooms and prophetic schools are great training grounds and great places to go out on a limb with a detailed prophetic word, but actually so is the world. The more we practice, the more we will recognize how God speaks to us. John Wimber said faith is spelled R-I-S-K!

REACH BEYOND YOUR COMFORT ZONE!

Simple Ways to Grow in the Prophetic:

- Want it
- Place a value upon it
- Become a friend of God, a Son and the Bride
- Begin each day in listening and talking with God
- Soaking, learn to quiet your mind
- Renew your mind with the Word
- Be filled with the Holy Spirit
- Sanctify your imagination
- Become heavenly minded
- Position yourself for prophetic encounters
- Make sure your motives are pure
- Walk in the fruit of the Holy Spirit
- Love above all
- Believe in the works that Jesus did
- Exercise and test your faith
- Intentionally build relationships with prophetic people
- Be teachable
- Be accountable to spiritual mentors
- Be sensitive to the voice of the Holy Spirit
- Trust the voice of the Holy Spirit
- Be obedient in the small things

Activation

Find 3 people to give a prophetic word to. Focus on what God is saying and release it with confidence. Of the three, no word should be the same.

Prophetic Challenge

Set the next week aside with daily, deep unto deep prayer. Go deeper, and become a friend of God.

NOTES

A Field Guide to Prophetic Ministry

OVERCOMING FEAR AND REJECTION

For God has not given us a spirit of fear, but of power and love and discipline (2 Timothy 1:7).

Everyone experiences a level of fear and rejection to some extent in their lives.

Rejection is usually the initial step. There is always a maturing process in prophetic ministry. Growing in the prophetic is a process in which we will make mistakes. The growth of our character is just as, if not more important than, growth in our prophetic gift. The prophetic words we speak may not be heard or understood by some and even be rejected.

We all are or have been "wounded soldiers" at some point. It is best to deal with our wounds quickly and completely. Contend for healing in the presence of God, who will carry all of our burdens and let them go. We all are like Jacob, walking with a limp, but when we let that limp become a compassion for others, our limp will become powerful! As we seek the Lord, He will send healing for our life wounds. SOZO** and other inner healing tools are also excellent ways to get free from our wounds.

**(For more info on SOZO, what it is and its function visit: www.tczion.com).

Rejection that is not healed may disguise itself as "discernment," but in reality, it will turn into suspicion, which can turn into fear, which can turn into isolation, bitterness, anger and so on.

We manifest fear because we do not want to experience rejection again. We must guard our heart and contend to walk in love. Perfect love casts out fear!

PROPHETIC GUIDELINES

The following guidelines are meant to help in exploring the prophetic, not become laws.

- We know in part, and we prophesy in part. (1 Corinthians 13:9)
- Be comfortable knowing that the prophetic word you give may not make sense to you.
- Eagerly desire to prophesy, in the right way.
- God speaks in many different ways and to people you may not expect. Learn to recognize the "voice of many waters."
- Be secure enough in yourself, knowing God made you in your unique way.
- The spirit of the prophets is subject to the prophets.
- Timing is essential. Some things should not be revealed, but prayed for.
- Try not to prophesy head knowledge.
- Prophesy from the motivation of God's love for the person.
- Prophesy with grace, gentleness and wisdom.
- Avoid negative prophecy; prophesy the solution not the problem.
- God may just give you a word or a sentence.
- Speak out only what God gives you to speak.
- Seek revelation, not your interpretation.
- Prophecy will never contradict the written Word.
- Follow the presence of the Lord. A good time to end the prophetic word is when HE leaves the conversation.
- A single word of destiny blessing can be more powerful than a 15 minute prophecy.
- Perform a "heart check" on yourself before giving a prophetic word.
- Your gift will make room for you; do not seek to establish yourself with your gift.
- Never try to control or manipulate anyone with the prophetic gift.
- Do not try to be the Holy Spirit to anyone.

- Don't prophesy beyond your faith.
- Practice, practice, practice your gift to expand your faith
- Overcome the fear of deception.
- Smile when you prophesy; God is in a good mood.
- Make decrees with authority.
- Breath mints are anointed. Knock them over with gift, not your breath.
- Use normal language, avoid King James English and Christianese. The words "Thus saith the Lord" are not necessary.
- Learn to become naturally supernatural.
- What God reveals, HE wants to heal.
- Search out people with a mature prophetic gift, and hang around them.
- Saturate yourselves with the prophetic experiences of others.
- Submit to authority in a personal mentoring relationship.
- Allow your prophetic words to be examined and tested, without taking offense.
- Always be humble.
- Do not allow denominational doctrines to influence the prophetic word.
- Prophetic evangelism is powerful.
- The power of Life and death are in your tongue; choose Life!

- An inaccurate prophetic word does not make that person a false prophet.
- Allow your mistakes and failures to be learning experiences.
- You will make mistakes, but God is bigger than your mistakes.
- Clean up your own messes. If you miss a word or said something in the moment that wasn't of God, you resolve it by going to the person and talking as laid out in Mathew 18.
- If a word involves direction, have an overseer involved in the application of the word.
- Prophecy can be a potential word and a conditional word.
- Strengthen, encourage and comfort.
- Invest in your prophetic education.
- Fear is a demonic spirit, defeat it in the name of Jesus.
- Resist condemnation. The enemy is an accuser.
- Resist the fear of making mistakes.
- Depend completely upon the Holy Spirit.

Final Thoughts

We have to always remember that prophecy and the prophetic ministry are not the prize, they are the means to the prize. The ultimate prize is God himself living on the inside of us, manifesting His nature through us. Don't be impressed with a gift, be continually impressed with His person, His nature, His love and His goodness. When we live in awe of Him, He will perpetually give us reason to be in awe. When we live in awe of our gift, or another's gift, it is exalting the sign above the very person the sign points to. Do not feel like you need to strive to earn a gift. He is a River that is flowing through you and it is as easy as simply letting Him flow. Let the work of the Holy Spirit move in us, on us and through us and we will be the ones who invite the world to "taste and see" that He is good!

> *Then he said to me, "This is the word of the Lord to Zerubbabel: Not by might, nor by power, but by my Spirit, says the Lord of hosts. (Zechariah 4:6)*

NOTES

NOTES

NOTES

NOTES

NOTES